BIM
MANAGEMENT
HANDBOOK

BIM Management Handbook

© RIBA Enterprises

Published by RIBA Publishing, part of RIBA Enterprises Ltd, The Old Post Office, St Nicholas
Street, Newcastle upon Tyne, NE1 1RH

ISBN 978 1 85946 605 6

Stock Code: 83973

British Library Cataloguing-in-Publication Data

A catalogue record for this book is available from the British Library.

Commissioning Editor: Sarah Busby
Production: Michèle Woodger
Designed, Typeset and Illustrated by HD-design
Cover design: Phil Handley
Printed and bound by WG Baird, United Kingdom

RIBA Publishing is part of RIBA Enterprises Ltd.

www.ribaenterprises.com

ABOUT THE AUTHOR AND CONTRIBUTORS

David Shepherd was BIM Manager at the London office of HOK Architects, a global practice of architects employing 16,000 people across 23 countries until 2015.

He is a fully trained BIM professional with 23 years' working experience of writing, presenting and implementing strategies for the design process automation of small and large architectural practices. His professional experience ranges from working as a qualified architectural technician in a major practice to CAD Manager, BIM Consultant and BIM Manager. HOK is a world leader in BIM and BuildingSMART.

Chapter 7 was contributed by Professor David Mosey PhD, Director of the Centre of Construction Law at King's College London. Professor Mosey was the Government's project mentor on the Cookham Wood Trial Project, which explored the combination of BIM Level 2 with early contractor involvement. He is author of Cabinet Office guidance on 'Two Stage Open Book and Supply Chain Collaboration', which illustrates how new procurement and contracting models can ensure that BIM delivers savings and improved value. Professor Mosey was formerly Head of Projects and Construction at Trowers & Hamlins solicitors, and won the 2009 Constructing Excellence Achiever's Award. He is author of the PPC2000 suite of partnering and alliancing contracts.

ACKNOWLEDGEMENTS

This book could not have been developed without the assistance of HOK International. In particular, HOK London, where I worked, was instrumental in allowing me time and other resources utilised in the preparation of this book, such as the stunning cover photo and vivid chapter opening images. These are representative of the outstanding project work that HOK has delivered through BIM across the world.

A sincere thanks to David King, the Technical Principal for HOK London, for his guidance and mentoring throughout the development of this book.

I also thank Professor David Mosey, Director of the Centre of Construction Law at King's College London, for the contribution of his legal expertise that he so ably demonstrated in writing Chapter 7.

I am also grateful to Alistair Kell, Director of Information Technology at BDP, who contributed guidance about the BIM Toolkit.

If, through the insights of this book, I have provided a partial glimpse into that future, it is because I have been standing on the shoulders of giants in this field of expertise. Consequently, I mention a few of the many official and informal mentors to whom I owe a debt of professional recognition and gratitude.

- Mark Bew, MBE
- William E. East, buildingSMART Alliance
- Stephen Hamil, NBS
- Alistair Kell, BDP
- David King, Technical Principal, HOK
- Patrick MacLeamy, CEO, HOK
- Lee Miller, HOK
- Professor David Mosey, UCL
- Nick Nisbet, AEC 3
- David Philp, AECOM
- Mervyn Richards, OBE
- Greg Schleusner, HOK
- Dale Sinclair, AECOM
- James Vandezande, HOK.

Finally and most importantly, I would like to thank my wife, Alison. Her supply of selfless encouragement and gracious sacrifice enabled me to finish this book.

This book may provide knowledge, but the gift of wisdom is divine:

'Wisdom is of utmost importance, therefore get wisdom, and, with all your effort, work to acquire understanding.'

(Proverbs 4:7)

TABLE OF CONTENTS

ABOUT THE AUTHOR AND CONTRIBUTORS, ACKNOWLEDGEMENTS   i

FOREWORD   v

01 THE CLIENT PERSPECTIVE: STRATEGY, COST AND LONG-TERM VALUE OF ASSET INFORMATION   7
Aligning BIM with the client's asset management strategy
From project cost to cost-in-use: Why clients seek to optimise cost-in-use
How post-construction BIM adds value

02 BUILDING BLOCKS FOR BIM DATA MANAGEMENT: STANDARDS, REQUIREMENTS AND PLANS   17
Employer's information requirements,
BIM execution plans, information delivery cycle,
Interoperability
Supply chain data collection,
Library management
Processes to validate data

03 ASSESSING YOUR PRACTICE AND GUIDING IT TO BIM-READINESS   37
Key BIM leadership roles and internal pre-BIM staff audit methods
Long-term strategic BIM goals for large and SME practices
Short-term BIM objectives: Monitoring progress towards results
Staffing the organisational roles for BIM
Software comparison and capabilities
The IT impact of BIM
Single and multi-firm BIM efficiency and effectiveness

04 BIM ADOPTION AND MATURITY LEVELS   51
3, 2, 1, Zero: What does BIM Maturity look like
Progressive goal setting for design collaboration in BIM

05 THE CHALLENGES AND BENEFITS OF BIM COORDINATION: 3D, 4D AND 5D   65
The practical use of BIM
How to signify and notify of design changes
The coordination team (Who?)
The spatial coordination meeting (Where?)
The sequence coordination meeting (When?)
The cost/quantification meeting (How much?)

06 MANAGING THE MANDATE: THE BIM LEVEL 2 ENVIRONMENT   81
What does BIM Level 2 mean?
Roles and staffing decisions
Model answers to the Plain Language Questions
Library management – standards and implementation
Software comparison and capabilities
What extra resources will we need?
Pairing technology with experience
Monthly, weekly and daily tasks

07 BIM AND CONTRACTS   95
The reasonable skill and care standard
Current procurement routes to collaboration
Reducing risk: Drawing exchange to model exchange
Specifying eliance on issued data: Level of Detail and Level of Information

08 BIM COLLABORATION AND WORKING WITHIN THE COMMON DATA ENVIRONMENT   107
Creating work in progress snapshots
Design verification procedures
Assigning and notifying of model Status
Capturing collaborative decisions in the model
Capturing design options in BIM
Value and design fixity in BIM
How to facilitate decision making through BIM

09 LEVEL OF DEFINITION PROGRESSION IN BIM   123
Agreeing the Level of Development progression
How LoD affects coordination
The importance of design sequence and fixity
Modelling access and clearances in 3D

10 BIM IN THE HAND-OVER PHASE   133
Why model contributions must be segregated (contractual/copyright boundaries)
PAS-1192 Model Federation: what it means and how it differs from model integration
Technologies and processes for integrating models
Maintaining models in tandem
Interoperability – what does it mean?
Aggregate model review processes
Processes to validate data: Model checking tools

CONCLUSION   142

GLOSSARY   144

INDEX   146

FOREWORD

Digital services are making all our lives simpler, faster and more connected. In most cases, this manifests itself into our everyday activities becoming more efficient. This same paradigm is now beginning to be realised in the construction sector where Building Information Modelling (BIM) is helping our industry to be more innovative, become more technologically advanced and create and care for our built assets and infrastructure.

As we make this shift to better modelling and managing our project information, it is important to give clear guidance to industry as to how they can mobilise or accelerate their journey towards Level 2 BIM maturity.

To some this journey can be daunting, transforming their ways of working and transactions from siloed and analogue to collaborative and digital. However, when properly unpacked the BIM process is axiomatic, allowing benefits to be unlocked at all stages of the asset life-cycle by both the client and the supply chain. This transformation is not simply about digital re-tooling, but also re-engineering processes, and most importantly building a framework of unified and collaborative working.

This handbook is an ideal guide to help anyone understand how BIM can help their business or project and practically create and implement a strategy for BIM. The book illustrates the importance of defining data to support project outcomes, especially to support efficiency beyond delivery and how these digital exchanges fit within the context of legal and commercial protocols for BIM. I am confident the BIM Management Handbook will support your transferal to BIM or move you further up the maturity wedge.

DAVID PHILP, HEAD OF BIM

01

THE CLIENT PERSPECTIVE:
STRATEGY, COST AND THE
LONG-TERM VALUE OF
ASSET INFORMATION

INTRODUCTION

In structuring this Handbook, it was important to think carefully about how best to balance the significant business needs of firms already employing a BIM Manager or Coordinator with those that have little or no BIM capability.

The starting point for Building Information Model management is the process of aligning your design technology strategy with not only the goals of your firm, but also those of your clients. This chapter captures why BIM is valuable to clients and how to formulate the BIM Strategy with added relevance to the client's own decision-making and asset management strategy.

The key coverage of this chapter is as follows;
- Building Information Modelling – a definition
- Where and why should we do BIM?
- BIM and Cost Analysis
- Defining BIM Objectives.

BUILDING INFORMATION MODELLING – A DEFINITION

In order to establish a common frame of reference, we begin by considering the formal industry definition of Building Information Modelling.

In the UK, the **Construction Project Information Committee** (CPIC) is a UK advisory group that has been a key participant in the development of common industry processes for BIM. Its BIM definition paraphrases that of the **US National Building Information Model Standard Project Committee,** stating:

'Building Information Modeling (BIM) is a digital representation of physical and functional characteristics of a facility. A BIM is a shared knowledge resource for information about a facility forming a reliable basis for decisions during its life-cycle; defined as existing from earliest conception to demolition'.[1]

WHY AND WHERE SHOULD WE DO 'BIM?'

Although we shall unpack this lengthy definition into simpler principles in the next few chapters, we shall now consider BIM in the light of the client's strategic priorities. Instead of repeating and refining existing definitions, this book begins by responding to the question that is often overlooked: *'Where and why should we do BIM?'*

In order to answer this, we should turn our attention to the overall purpose of innovation as a means of business improvement. Typically, new technology is adopted to deliver enhanced value with greater efficiency. So, BIM strategy should provide greater value to the client and your organisation as well as improving project efficiency.

In simple terms, BIM allows users to share project and asset information by mapping that data onto 3D representations of building components that reside in the model. Combining shared models aggregates the mapped data so that users can review, sort and filter the combined and comprehensive inputs of all project participants.

For instance, by selecting a plant room space in the plan, users can review its dimensions established by the architect, the air flows needed to maintain the required room temperatures (known as set points), the boiler's clearances as set by the building service engineer and the self-weight assigned to the same equipment by the structural engineer.

The value of BIM is in providing a graphical environment in which all of the specialised data for any area or element in the proposed building is immediately accessible to all users.

Of course, as with any other business system, information loses value when it becomes inaccessible, out of date or erroneous. This is true of all collaborative data development Yet, considering the many other databases that businesses employ, such a truism does not make the case for not using them.

CONSIDERING THE CLIENT'S LONG RANGE BUSINESS GOALS

While it's always useful to focus on project-specific goals, doing so to the neglect of the client's long–range business strategy is unwise. Such an approach places undue emphasis on the relatively short-lived value that can be extracted during the project lifecycle, whereas it is far better to also tap into the long-term priorities of both current and prospective clients.

The other consequence of pursuing a solely project-based approach to BIM is that it becomes overly focused on the 'what' and 'how' of each process rather than *why* a particular output is needed in the first place. It is all too easy to concentrate on the mechanisms involved in delivering every imaginable kind of BIM output without first determining which deliverables are of sufficiently compelling value to both the project and client.

THE IMPORTANCE OF RELATING BIM STRATEGY TO CLIENT STRATEGY

If BIM is not aligned with the client's business priorities, the strategy for implementing it will become skewed towards just improving internal and collaborative efficiency, instead of maximising its overall effectiveness on behalf of the client. Instead, BIM strategy should, within the constraints of available time and resources, aim to maximise the value of the technology for both the client and the project team.

ALIGNMENT WITH CLIENT ASSET MANAGEMENT STRATEGY

To this end, consulting the client's asset management strategy is a useful starting point for developing an all-encompassing BIM strategy.

Consider a major food retailer that sets a goal of opening 150 new branded high street stores across the country over the next three years. While major project-related costs will be incurred by that decision, associated with that corporate priority is the significantly higher long-term impact on operations, maintenance and disposal costs.

It is because of the relatively higher costs incurred in use and beyond the immediate project lifecycle that a comprehensive BIM strategy must reflect the asset management strategy of the client. Note that this is very different from attempting to consult the client's own BIM strategy (assuming that one exists).

As an example, consider this excerpt from the UK's Network Rail Asset Management Strategy. The Executive Summary explains: *'Network Rail's commitment to its customers is enshrined in a Promise to deliver the Timetable, so that trains run safely, punctually and reliably – now and in increasing numbers in the future. Asset Management supports the delivery of the Promise by planning, delivering and making available an infrastructure that supports the current and future timetable – safely, efficiently and sustainably.'* [2]

It is important to note that the stated approach is in support of the rail infrastructure operator's business commitment. The emphasis is on achieving infrastructure availability capable of supporting the Network Rail's promise to deliver current and expanding future timetable requirements. This goal is qualified by the importance of maintaining safety (which is reiterated), efficiency and sustainability. Later in this document, there is also recognition that *'a significant improvement in our asset management capability is required to live up to this commitment'*.

So, it would be neglectful for the design team to adopt a strategy that bypasses Network Rail's asset management goals.

Further along in the Network Rail Strategy document, the importance of the asset management strategy is clarified: *'Asset management of the railway infrastructure is fundamentally about delivering the outputs valued by our customers and funders and other key stakeholders, in a sustainable way, for the lowest whole life cost.'*

So, in this case, whatever your internal priorities for BIM, the client's stated asset management goal, like this one, should shape your long-term BIM strategy. Therefore, one of the client-aligned BIM goals for an infrastructure contractor working on Network Rail projects might read: *'To provide BIM outputs that enable key stakeholders to ascertain readily the impact on asset value of our design and construction alternatives and determine the lowest sustainable whole life cost as design proceeds.'*

As another example, consider a Housing Association that has implemented a strategic goal that aims to *'identify a five per cent increase in the overall net present value (NPV) of our property asset base, extracting maximum value for those assets whilst supporting a diverse portfolio to ensure mixed communities.'*

Net present value takes inflation into account by discounting costs incurred over the building's lifecycle in order to price them in today's money. In the graph below, the annual increases in operations and maintenance (O and M) costs are depicted by the orange bars, while the purple bars represent their respective net present values.

Figure 1.1 Lifecycle operations and maintenance costs

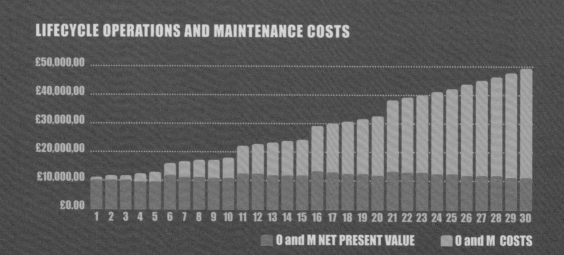

Given that the Housing Association's goal is a five percent overall increase in net present value, this could be achieved by either gross rental increases, or by reducing the operations and maintenance costs by the same amount.

Here is a corresponding BIM goal that would garner their interest: *'By means of BIM analysis, to optimise sustainable design strategies in order to deliver a consistent five percent reduction on baseline O and M lifecycle cost projections'.* Once achieved, this forms a far more likely basis for repeat business with the Association than just streamlining the drawing production process.

As a final example, the Education Funding Agency has implemented a set of non-statutory area guidelines for mainstream schools. In furtherance of this guidance, it has also issued a spreadsheet-based Schedule of Accommodation reporting tool for ensuring that the spaces, as designed, fall within the area ranges (based on group sizes) specified in Building Bulletin 103.

In addition, standardised area data sheet (ADS) codes are used to classify the wide variety of classroom types and room functions.

Figure 1.2 Education Funding Agency's Schedule of Accommodation tool.

date [ ]   age range **3-11**   school name **Primary SoA tool v6.2 template**   as a check:

	classes				net capacity	
reception places **60**	2	net capacity		type of school **community**		net capacity for recommended
infant places **120**	4	for SoA below = **420**		site: area (m²) [ ] type **ample site**		SoA below: **420**
junior places **240**	8	within a potential range of:		existing buildings: type **none (all new)**		
FTE age 3-4 nursery places **52**	14	**378** to **420**		19 m²float not over gross		**378** to **420**
Total Mainstream Places **472**	**420**	4 to 11 places				recommended

Additionally resourced FTE places for:
aged 2 to 3 **nursery FTE** [ ]
- **SEN** [ ]

organisation options for:
infant **all practical in classrooms**
junior **specialist practical spaces**

ADS code		max. group size	average area of space (m²)	TOTAL no. of spaces	TOTAL AREA (m²)	SUPP AREA (m2)		recommended area of space (m²)	no. of spaces
	Basic Teaching Area		(16)						
PRI03	nursery playroom	27	55	2	110		54 m2 or 2.3m2 per place min recom'd	55	2
PRI13	reception classroom	30	62	2	124		62 m2 minimum recommended	62	2
PRI36	shared teaching area with sink	35	62	4	248		62 m2 minimum recommended	62	4
PRI33	junior classroom	30	55	8	440		55 m2 minimum recommended	55	8
	specialist practical/ other								
PRA12	food/ science/ DT area	30	62	1	62			62	1
	food/ science/ DT area								
	infant food/ science/ DT area								
	TOTAL AREA min **960** max **1087**				984		OK: area within recommended range	984	
	Large spaces: halls, studios and dining						dining options 60 mins all in main hall		
HAL13	main hall (primary) assembly max	350	180	1	180		105 m² min. recom'd for all pupils dining	180	1
HAL11	studio	30	55	1	55			55	1
	small hall	30	80					80	
	TOTAL AREA min **226** max **272**				235		OK: area within recommended range	235	
	Learning Resource Areas								
LIB01	library	20	34	1	34		30 m² minimum recommended	34	1
SEN01	SEN resource base	5	12	1	12			12	1
SEN11	SEN therapy/ MI room	5	12	1	12			12	1
RES00	small group room	4	9	3	27			9	3
RES00	small group room (nursery)	4	9	2	18			9	2
	TOTAL AREA min **57** max **124**				103		OK: area within recommended range	103	
	Staff and Administration Areas								
OFF31	staff room (prep and social)	22	41	1	41		51 m² min total staff area recom'd	41	1
OFF33	staff work room	4	13	1	13			13	1
ADM11	head's office (meeting room)	6	16	1	16			16	1
OFF10	office/ meeting room	3	9	1	9			9	1
OFF35	staff work room (with sink)	-	11	1	11		11 m2 recom'd for nursery incl kitchen	11	1
	staff work (specially resourced)	-							
ADM05	general office (1 recep desk)	4	20	1	20			20	1
ADM08	reprographics room	-	11	1	11			11	1
ADM01	entrance/ reception		5	1	5		net area of this space only	5	1

In alignment with this official guidance, the corresponding BIM goal would be: *'To facilitate the review of design options by automating the production of area data sheets from BIM and thereby significantly reducing the requirement for manual data entry to complete standardised Schedule of Accommodation reports.'*

WHY SHOULD ASSET COST CONSIDERATIONS BE IMPORTANT TO YOUR BIM STRATEGY?

The costs associated with a proposed asset are key to the client's determination about whether it will meet their performance requirements. In particular, whole life costing seeks to provide a consistent basis for comparing the long-term impact of alternative proposals that require different cash flows over different timeframes.

If an organisation's BIM strategy does not seek to facilitate these long-term asset cost comparisons, it will miss the opportunity for using the technology to facilitate and influence the client's investment decisions. BIM is a technology that provides for direct integration of financially valuable data with design or construction proposals. A good example of this capability is the automatic production of Gross Internal Floor Area schedules from the model.

In respect of long-term feasibility, it is important to distinguish initial capital expenditure (CAPEX) from ongoing operating expenditure (OPEX). To consider the former without regard to the latter would lead to short-sighted investment decisions that have no long-term viability.

One method of reviewing both CAPEX and OPEX involves assessing the Whole Life Cost including Life Cycle Cost. The components that together comprise Whole Life Cost are shown in fig. 1.4

Project No:		Project Name:		Room Data Sheet No: SS2		Rev No:	
Principal Function: A general purpose teaching space not requiring specialist environments. eg. English, Maths, MFL, History, Geography, RE general Studies. Personal Health & Social Studies.							
Area: See table of room functions & sizes		**Date:**		**Room Name:** Classroom			
Critical Adjacencies: Access to shared facilities, storage and toilet facilities.							

Finishes & Fittings	Mechanical		Electrical				
Floor: natural fibre carpet, suitable for use with ICT equipment.	**Design Temp:**	18°c	Double 13 amp Sockets: RCB protected	12no	**Emergency Lighting:**		*
Skirting: softwood FSC timber.	**Emitter Type:** radiators, underfloor heating or fan convectors.	yes	**Door Power:**	no	**Fire Alarm System:** (sounder to be audible from room)		*
Wall: smooth decorative finish. Pin boards equivalent to 6 no. 2.4mx1.2m sheets.	**Natural/Passive Vent:** see BB 101	yes	**Window Power:** Only to clerestory and/or rooflights with rain sensors.	no	**Heat Detector:**		*
Ceiling: min. height 2.7m, light reflective finish with access to concealed services.	**Mechanical Vent:**	no	**Data & Comms:** (single outlet)	yes 20no	**Break Glass:**		*
Door Type: solid core flush door with observation panel and paint ply finish.	**Cooling:**	no	**TV:**	no	**Smoke Detector:**		*
Ironmongery: suited door lock/s. SAA ironmongery to internal door/s and windows.	**Hot Water:**	no	**Ceiling Projector:** (Complete with audio outlets only)	yes	**Audio/Visual Alarm:**		no
F&F included in Contract: Fix only: whiteboard 2.4x1.2m. supply & fix: Dim out blinds or curtains (inc. roof lights) 6 lin. m. of adjustable shelving. Fire fighting equipment*.	**Cold Water:**	no	**Lighting Level:** 300lux at 0.8m above FFL.		**Intruder Detector (PIR):** CCTV facilities		** no
	Drinking Water:	no	**Type:** Low energy with uplighting capability, suitable for IT use within the area. Daylight dimming required wherever appropriate.		**Security/Disabled Alarm:**		no
F & F excluded from Contract: Whiteboard and Clock.	**Gas Supply:**	no			**Electric Locking:**		no
Telephone handset, Projector, audio equipment/interactive white board supplied & installed by Schools contractor.			**Feature:** to whiteboard	yes	**Student Registration:**		no
			Switching: automatic with PIR Sensors complete with blackout Override switch.	yes	**Public Address System:**		no
	Health & Safety				**Telephone:**		yes
	Restrictor stays on all windows with low sills below 1100mm. Shelving to be max of 1750mm above ffl, support uprights max of 1900mm above ffl.				**Hearing Enhancement:** Sound Field System facility to be available in at least one classroom		yes
					Drama Lighting:		no
					*dependent on 'Fire Strategy' **dependent on 'Intruder Strategy'		

Additions/Omissions to above requested by Client:		Notes Refer to Building Bulletin 92: Modern and Foreign Languages Accommodation, for MFL classrooms.	
SS2 / RDS 04/08	**Approved By:** Client: Date:	End User: Date:	Other: Date:

Figure 1.3   Sample school area data sheet (Courtesy of Cornwall Council)

Whole Life Cost predictions are crucial to the process for gaining financial authorisation for a building project, as it proceeds through distinct decision-making stages, known as **gateways.** At these gateways, stakeholders participate in reviews to assess the business case and technical feasibility of a project before approving further work.

It's important to remember that money tied up in a construction project, or in operating the resulting asset, could have been profitably invested or lent elsewhere. Therefore, it is important for businesses to evaluate the potential returns on those investment alternatives that are being rejected in favour of a particular scheme. As a consequence, the importance of assigning monetary value to the significant resources expended in producing or maintaining an asset cannot be understated.

In order to assign costs to projects through BIM, elements in the model are classified by a set of common building functions, such as roof, enclosure and structural frame. By means of export to a compatible database format, the model's data structure provides comprehensive schedules of quantities and can also be embedded with historical cost data as a starting point for O and M cost estimates. As the designers update their models with

alternatives, the schedules and estimates will automatically update to provide a faster means of comparison with the cost plan.

BIM AND COST ANALYSIS

The Building Cost Information Service (BCIS) of the Royal Institution of Chartered Surveyors provides the **Elemental Standard Form of Cost Analysis**[5] (SFCA) as the definitive industry-wide standard for cost planning. In accordance with the New Rules of Measurement 2, the document assigns the different components of building design to 14 categories of element definitions for costing purposes. In each case, the SFCA document clarifies the rules and units of measurement.

A logical consequence of these definitions is that if quantities derived from our models are not structured in accordance with these definitions, they will not facilitate useful comparison.

So, a consequent (and often neglected) goal of a design or construction firm's BIM strategy would be: *'To consistently classify models and quantities derived from them in alignment with industry-standard elemental cost definitions, thereby facilitating a significantly more detailed and useful response to the Client's Cost Plan reviews.'*

Figure 1.4 Whole Life Cost breakdown – ISO 15686-5[4]

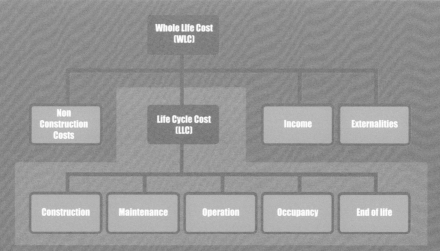

DEFINING BIM OBJECTIVES

There is also a further need to break each goal down into several short-range objectives that allow us to evaluate the trajectory for success. These milestones should be specific, measurable, achievable, realistic and timely (for which the business acronym is SMART). They punctuate the journey towards achieving each strategic goal.

For instance, it is of immense value for client decision-making to be improved by BIM through transparency about costs (both project and whole life). This would be the impetus for a number of BIM objectives:

- *'To automate the classification of model elements for industry-standard cost analysis in accordance with the BCIS Standard Form of Cost Analysis (SFCA) for all projects by year 2 of our BIM implementation programme.'*

- *'By year 3, to develop in conjunction with cost consultants a reliable method of applying BCIS pricing to BCIS structured schedules of quantities derived from BIM, thereby allowing stakeholders to readily compare the cost of design alternatives against the Cost Plan.'*

Achieving these objectives will involve tactical choices discussed later in this book. Nevertheless, the proviso for achieving collaborative objectives is a well-defined contractual arrangement that ensures that all project participants understand the terms under which this information is being shared.

BIM STRATEGY AND THE LONG-TERM VALUE OF ASSET INFORMATION:

Value can be understood as the economic benefit that is derived from a product or service. The key benefits of asset information are outlined in PAS-55, the Publicly Available Specification for the Management of Physical Assets.

This accepted UK Standard explains of asset data that:[6]

'Examples of information to be considered include the following:

- *Descriptions of assets, their functions and the asset system they serve*
- *Unique asset identification numbers;*
- *Locations of the assets, possibly using spatial referencing or geographical information systems*
- *The criticality of assets to the organisation;*
- *Details of ownership and maintenance demarcation where assets interface across a system or network of assets*
- *Engineering data, design parameters, and engineering drawings*
- *Details of asset dependencies and interdependencies*
- *Vendor data (details of the organisation that supplied the asset)*
- *Commissioning dates and data*
- *The condition and duty of assets*
- *Condition and performance targets or standards*
- *Key performance indicators*
- *Asset related standards, process(es) and procedure(s)'.*

In particular, it also states that: *'asset management information should be capable of enabling an organisation to:*

- *Make life cycle cost comparisons of alternative capital investments*
- *Determine the total cost of maintaining a specific asset(s)/asset system*
- *Identify expiry of warranty period and warranty*
- *Comply with statutory and regulatory obligations*
- *Obtain/calculate asset replacement values*
- *Determine the end of economic life of assets/asset systems, e.g. the point in time when the asset related expenditure exceeds the associated income.'* [6]

Therefore, in respect of these capabilities, another key goal of BIM strategy would be defined as: *'To develop and demonstrate the capability to deliver asset information from BIM in a structure compatible with PAS-55 compliant industry-standard asset information management processes.'*

The reason for defining the goal as being to *'develop and demonstrate the capability'* is that the delivery of such information would generally only make sense when it applies to an agreed contractual obligation, positions the firm to win significantly more business or represents added value for which the client will pay a premium.

CHECKLIST FOR FORMULATING YOUR BIM STRATEGY:

In formulating your own BIM Strategy, take a look at the headline goals in the asset management strategies of major clients and ask yourself the following questions.

- How do your current goals for design and BIM align with your client asset management strategy?

- Can you describe the asset management strategy of your firm's largest client? Where does that information exist?

- Where and how have cost planning and asset information been introduced as key goals of your BIM strategy?

- Beyond graphical and textual output for design and construction, what initial considerations about the long-term value of the data from BIM could you provide for the client at handover?

- How will the client be able to sustain the value to their own business of the data that you intend to hand over?

- Has the client adequately planned resources for updating that data over the life of the facility?

- Have you investigated which software file formats will ensure your project data is readily accessible and appropriate to your client's short- and long-term business requirements?

CONCLUSION

We have reviewed the importance of formulating the firm's BIM Strategy from the standpoint of your client's own strategy. This client focus should be balanced with internal and collaborative project goals for BIM. Nevertheless, if the strategy does not recognise the client's priorities, it will fail to encompass the full business potential of BIM.

[1] National Building Information Modeling Standard (2007), (National Institute of Building Sciences: United States), p.21
[2] Staying on the Right Track – Case Study (2014), (Institute of Asset Management: United Kingdom)
[3] Building Bulletin 103, 2014© (Crown copyright)
[4] BS ISO 15686-5 Buildings and constructed assets. Service life planning. Life cycle costing, 2008 (BSI: United Kingdom)
[5] Elemental Standard Form of Cost Analysis, 4th Edition, 2012 (Building Cost Information Service of the Royal Institution of Chartered Surveyors, RICS: United Kingdom)
[6] PAS 55-2:2008 Asset Management Part 2, 2008 (Institute of Asset Management: United Kingdom), p.28

02

BUILDING BLOCKS FOR BIM DATA MANAGEMENT: STANDARDS, REQUIREMENTS AND PLANS

INTRODUCTION

In this chapter, we review the best practice guidance of the BIM Task Group (an advisory group established by the UK Government and comprising representatives of major UK construction industry institutions), which has developed nationally recognised standards, forms and processes for preparing production and asset information from BIM.

The Group's recommended approach involves a 'Push-Pull' mechanism. This means that, as part of the pre-qualification process, the client issues its predefined requirements for the delivery from BIM of coordinated data that will inform its decision to proceed through each project stage (Push). In turn, the supplier (i.e. the lead designer or main contractor) is responsible for coordinating the aggregation of information extracted from the combined models of the entire supply chain in order to meet those requirements in a timely fashion (Pull).

We will explore the significance and format of the Employer's Information Requirements (EIRs). The response to these EIRs is the provision of a BIM method statement, known as the Pre-Contract BIM Execution Plan.

Once the contract is awarded, the resources and plans for information delivery are confirmed through the supplier's provision of the Post-Contract BIM Execution Plan.

The key coverage of this chapter is as follows;
* The context of the Government Construction Strategy: BIM Level 2 and PAS-1192
* Employer's Information Requirements
* The Pre-Contract BIM Execution Plan
* The Post-Contract BIM Execution Plan
* Information Delivery Plans.

THE CONTEXT OF THE GOVERNMENT CONSTRUCTION STRATEGY: BIM LEVEL 2 AND PAS-1192

The UK Government announced its Construction Strategy in May 2011. While some of its cost reduction approaches were devoted to improved payment and procurement methods, the most innovative proposal was for all centrally procured projects to adopt fully collaborative 3D BIM – also known as BIM level 2 – by 2016.

BIM LEVEL 2

Level 2 Maturity is defined in the Department for Business, Innovation and Skill's BIM Working Party strategy paper as:

'A managed 3D environment held in separate discipline "BIM" tools with data attached. Commercial data will be managed by enterprise resource planning software and integrated by proprietary interfaces or bespoke middleware. This level of BIM may utilise 4D construction sequencing and/or 5D cost information.' [1]

We shall clarify the meaning of 4D, 5D and other dimensions of BIM in Chapter 5. However, at this stage, the BIM Level 2 mandate establishes the importance of delivering information from the model(s) in accordance with predefined requirements.

PAS-1192

The PAS-1192 documentation is a suite of specifications introduced as a consequence of the Government's BIM Strategy. Together, they provide guidance for collaborative project/asset information management through BIM. PAS-1192-2 describes the generic BIM workflows that should be adapted to the distinctive design, construction and asset management requirements of specific building projects.

That strategy was informed by the commissioned BIM Working Party strategy paper issued earlier that year, which established the importance of two overarching strategic actions: Client 'Push' and (in response to this) Project Team 'Pull.'[2]

EMPLOYERS' INFORMATION REQUIREMENTS

CLIENT PUSH AND SUPPLIER PULL

In terms of 'Push', the same paper emphasised:

'The Government client should be very specific and consistent about what it specifies. This includes the need to specify a set of information (data) to be provided by the supply chain to the client at specific times through the delivery and operational life of the asset.'[3]

It is with this in mind that PAS-1192-2[4] identifies the Employer's Information Requirements (EIRs) as the means by which clients specify the information that the lead designer and main contractor are expected to provide via BIM. For all public works, EIRs are used to explain what kind of data is needed from BIM and when it should be provided. In effect, the pre-contract EIRs constitute a consistently structured Request for Proposals relating to BIM.

Figure 2.1 The Push-Pull Strategy for BIM

CLIENT 'PUSH'
(Employers' Information Requirements)

PROJECT TEAM 'PULL'
(BIM Project Execution Planning and Information Delivery through BIM)

When preparing their EIRs, the extent of the client's reliance on the advice of independent technical advisers will typically depend on the level of internal BIM expertise. Where the client finds that little or no such expertise is available internally, they should, at the earliest opportunity, consult an external adviser with a verifiable track record of successful BIM implementations and client satisfaction.

In addition, while the design team leader or main contractor may be well positioned to provide support in compiling the EIRs, an undesirable level of self-policing may result from appointing either of these figures to develop the self-same EIRs that will be applied to their proposed design and construction processes. The appointment of a party entirely separate from the project team to the role of BIM Technical Adviser on these matters would ensure greater accountability.

The EIRs can be broadly divided into the following Technical, Management and Commercial Requirements:[5]

TECHNICAL REQUIREMENTS	MANAGEMENT REQUIREMENTS	COMMERCIAL REQUIREMENTS
• Software Platforms	• Standards Deliverables	• Data Drops and Project
• Data Exchange Format	• Roles and Responsibilities	• Clients Strategic Purpose
• Coordinates	• Planning the Work and Data Segregation	• Defined BIM/Project Deliverables
• Level of Detail	• Security	• BIM-specific Competence Assessment
• Training	• Coordination and Clash Detection Process	
	• Collaboration Process	
	• Health and Safety and Construction Design Management	
	• Systems Performance	
	• Compliance Plan	
	• Delivery Strategy for Asset Information	

Table 2.1 Showing sub-sections of the Employer's Information Requirements

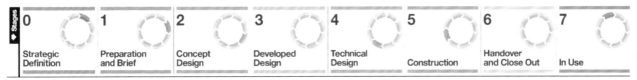

Stages							
0 Strategic Definition	**1** Preparation and Brief	**2** Concept Design	**3** Developed Design	**4** Technical Design	**5** Construction	**6** Handover and Close Out	**7** In Use

Figure 2.2   The stages of the RIBA Plan of Work 2013

THE RIBA PLAN OF WORK AND PLAIN LANGUAGE QUESTIONS

The RIBA Plan of Work[6] consistently organises the building design and construction process into a series of work stages.

At each juncture between these stages, it is important for clients to decide on whether the project is sufficiently viable for it to continue. The EIRs specify the format and quality of data that must be delivered from BIM in order to answer the client's important questions about project progress. These predefined queries, designed to solicit formal responses from the delivery team, are phrased in everyday English and therefore termed the Plain Language Questions.

In summary, the EIRs establish a consistent digital format for providing data that can be reviewed by the client in order to assess and approve the project's progress and viability at each work stage. The common term for the formal project review and approval process is the Gateway.

The UK Government's BIM Task Group has provided examples of typical Plain Language Questions that would be posed at each work stage, along with the expected format of responses via BIM (see http://www.thenbs. com/BIMTaskGroupLabs/questions.html). The samples below relate to the RIBA Plan of Work, Stage 1: Preparation and Brief (corresponding to American Institute of Architects Phase 1).

REVIEWING THE BUSINESS IMPACT OF EIRS

There are significant responsibilities involved in meeting the expectations contained in EIRs for information delivery via BIM. For each requirement, the BIM Manager should assess the contractual scope and the risks incurred by the specified information requirements,

PLAIN LANGUAGE QUESTION	RESPONSE VIA BIM
How are the stakeholders' needs captured?	An electronic brief that is in a format that may be used for automated validation of proposals.
What is the initial view of capital cost?	3D model of the development's volumes. Schedule of internal volumes, land, floor, wall and roof areas or service runs aligned with generic cost data as aggregated by the cost estimator. Fabric not normally represented. Budget breakdown.

Table 2.2   Examples of Plain Language Questions and the BIM-derived responses to them

EIR RISK ASSESSMENT CHECKLIST:

1   What are the overall strategic purposes of BIM specified in the EIRs for this project?

2   Which specific uses of BIM have been prioritised for this project?

3   What is the contractual significance of the model vis-à-vis the issued drawings?

4   How is the intellectual property embedded in each firm's model contractually protected?

5   At each project stage, how does the required level of detail and information relate to each firm's contractual scope?

6   Prior to commencement, what sort of digital data (e.g. site survey, electronic Schedule of Accommodations) will be provided? What are their file formats?

7   What can be discovered about the proven capabilities of other firms in the supply chain to collaborate, coordinate and deliver information from BIM in accordance with the EIRs?

8   How will any lack of BIM proficiency be remediated before or during the project?

9   What are the existing software, processes and tools that will be employed in accordance with the EIRs?

10 Which EIRs would demand a significant change over from existing tools, deliverables and work methods?

11 Which requirements are unnecessarily onerous and, on that basis, should be open to amendment?

and devise a careful plan to mitigate them. In terms of the EIRs that accompany bid documentation, it is invaluable to conduct a comprehensive risk assessment that draws upon the experience and insight of the BIM Manager. A checklist like the one above is a useful tool when assessing this risk.

In respect of question 11, an important step would be for the assigned Project Manager and the person assuming the BIM management role to invite the client's BIM Technical Adviser to explain the purpose of any particularly challenging requirements, with a view to achieving an acceptable compromise.

Understanding the risks incurred by these requirements, finding the compromises that will mitigate them, and persuading the client to approve such amendments are all key aspects of pre-contract BIM management. They are at least as important as the technical requirements that you will specify, should you recruit a person to perform this role.

THE PRE-CONTRACT BIM EXECUTION PLAN

PAS-1192-2 describes the Pre-Contract BIM Execution Plan (BEP) as a coherent proposal that establishes the prospective design and construction supply chain's strategy and

Figure 2.3 The Five Components of the Pre-Contract BIM Project Execution Plan

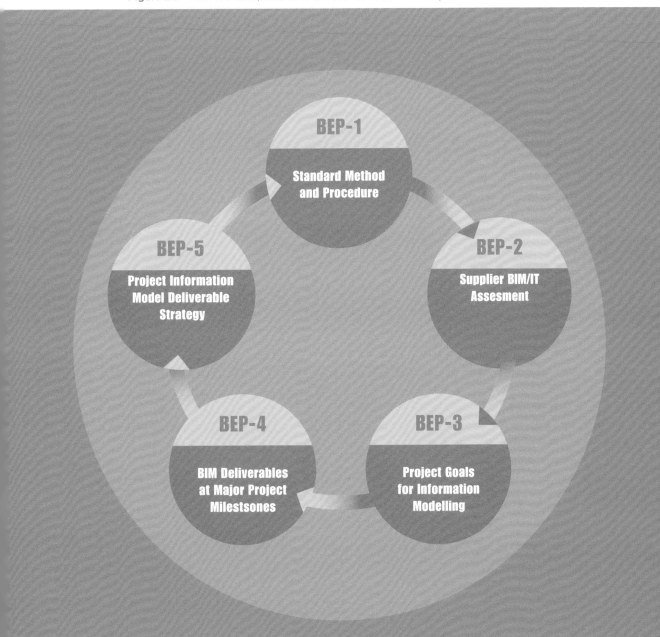

SELF-TEST QUESTIONS THAT WILL HELP YOU TO COMPLETE THE PAS-1192-RELATED ASSESSMENT FORMS:

1   Describe the significance of BIM to your normative design/construction collaboration processes. What high-level business improvements (e.g. cost, time and quality) have you been seeking to derive from BIM?

2   What objective criteria are you using to measure those improvements?

3   Where and how have you objectively defined your firm's CAD/BIM Standards?

4   How stringently does your firm check its project documentation against those CAD/BIM Standards?

5   Identify three of your firm's most successful project implementations of BIM. Describe the range of design and construction functions in which BIM was used. How did BIM improve project outcomes, in terms of cost, time and quality?

6   What's your experience of administering or using a Common Data Environment for the multi-disciplinary team to share?

capability to deliver the information as required by the Employer from BIM.

The diagram on the facing page shows the five key components comprising the plan.

In the subsequent section, each component of the BIM Project Execution Plan will be explained in terms of what it means and what it should contain:

BEP - 1 – THE STANDARD METHOD AND PROCEDURE

The **Standard Method and Procedure** should encompass proposals for:

- Roles and responsibilities, in particular the overall responsibility for BIM coordination and information delivery from the full range of design and construction disciplines.

- A secure online repository of shared project models and data known as the Common Data Environment (defined in PAS-1192-2 as '*a single source of information for any given project, used to collect, manage and disseminate all relevant approved project documents for multi-disciplinary teams in a managed process*).'

- Compatible software applications for model development and file formats required for information exchange.

- Common conventions for file and folder naming that would make it easy to distinguish the originator, discipline, zone, level, purpose and revision status assigned to each model.

- The means by which the Common Data Environment will logically segregate work-in-progress models from shared data and client-approved construction documentation.

It's important to note that the primary purpose of BIM Level 2 is coordinated information management and not just the management of coordinated *drawing* production.

BEP - 2 – SUPPLIER BUILDING INFORMATION MANAGEMENT, IT AND RESOURCE ASSESSMENT

In response to the BIM-related aspects of any bid documentation, the BIM Manager will also be expected to complete a number of PAS-1192-related assessment forms on behalf of his/her firm. The responses on these forms should provide evidence-based confirmation of:

- Understanding of BIM and its applicability to the normative design/construction collaboration processes of the firm
- The design and construction functions for which BIM has been utilised and the successful project outcomes attributed to it
- IT, training/assessment and management provisions in place for project delivery in BIM
- Current processes for vetting work against CAD/BIM standards
- The extent to which the firm's CAD/BIM Standards are aligned with national BIM standards
- Successful implementations of BIM on key projects.

These are probing questions, but answering them candidly will go a long way towards ascertaining your company's BIM Level 2 readiness.

BEP - 3 – PROJECT GOALS FOR COLLABORATION AND INFORMATION MODELLING

Project goals represent the outcomes by which we measure the success of using BIM.

Let's return to the Government Construction Strategy and remind ourselves of the key benefits that it cites for adopting BIM:

- Comparative ease in evaluating the implications of alternative design proposals
- Elimination of coordination errors and subsequent expensive change because projects are modelled in three dimension.
- Elimination of unnecessary intermediaries by linking design to manufacture by direct control of machine tools
- Establishing a proper basis for asset management subsequent to construction.

In a fully collaborative 3D environment, BIM Level 2 involves the extraction of the commercial data that has been cross-referenced to 3D elements located in the various model contributions of each discipline. In short, once the appropriate kind of data is attached to the model elements, the client should be able to use proprietary tools to extract further information from them; this information can then be analysed in order to assess and even improve project outcomes.

In line with these kinds of benefits, project goals should be described in accordance with the EIRs. Here are a few examples:

- *'In conjunction with other consultants, BIM will be used to facilitate the client's evaluation of design alternatives by providing 3D visualisations of different proposals with associated cost estimates, area schedules and energy usage projections.'*

- *'BIM will be used to significantly reduce the cost of design re-work by using collaborative model walkthroughs, whereby all design issues raised by consultants will be mapped to specific elements and named views of the model. Potential conflicts will be resolved by using the combined 3D model to coordinate a solution that is agreeable to all relevant parties.'*

- *'BIM will be used to make the construction process faster and safer by developing and reviewing construction sequence animations and Design for Manufacture and Assembly proposals developed from the 3D models.'*

- *'At handover, BIM will be used to provide a comprehensive verified set of asset information in a format compatible with the client's FM system.'*

Of course, these goals may incur significant immediate additional costs that will be offset by consequent savings and benefits realised later on in the project lifecycle. These need to be negotiated against the contractual scope of project participants.

BEP - 4 – MAJOR PROJECT MILESTONES CONSISTENT WITH THE PROJECT PROGRAMME

The table below shows the types of deliverables that would be derived from BIM for client review at the end of each project stage.

BEP - 5 – PROJECT INFORMATION MODEL (PIM) DELIVERABLE STRATEGY

As a deliverable, the Project Information Model integrates actionable project data and documentation with progressively more detailed elements in the 3D model.

In its document entitled *Outline Scope of Services for the Role of information Management*[7], the Construction Industry Council (CIC) refers to this PIM deliverables strategy as the Project Information Plan, calling it *'the plan for the structure and management and exchange of information from the Project Team in the Information Model and the related processes and procedures.'*

It adds that the plan should contain:

a) Responsibility for provision of information at each Stage

b) Level of detail/information required for specific Project Outputs e.g. Planning, Procurement, FM Procurement

c) Information structure across roles e.g. software platforms (all levels of supply chain) and data structures (also known as the data schema) appropriate to the employer requirements and project team resources

PROJECT STAGE	STRATEGIC DEFINITION - 0	PREPARATION & BRIEF - 1	CONCEPT DESIGN - 2	DEVELOPED DESIGN - 3	TECHNICAL DESIGN - 4	CONSTRUCTION - 5	HAND-OVER/ CLOSE OUT - 6
Deliverables	BEP Review	BEP Review	BEP Review	BEP Review	BEP Review	BEP Review	BEP Review
	Models: Electronic brief in a format that can be used to automatically validate proposals	Models: Architectural Massing; Civil	Models :Arch.; Civil; Structural w. Analytical input; MEP w. plant and primary service routes; Specialty Consultants	Models: Arch; Civil; Structural (Analytical); MEP w. primary and secondary; Specialty Consultants; CAD Files	Models: Arch; Civil; Structural (Analytical); MEP w. detailed connections; Specialty Consultants; CAD Files	Models: Constructional; Coordination; Shop Drawing; Fabrication; Scheduling and Phasing; Record Drawings	Models: Concurrent 'As-Built'; All As-Built Coordination and Fabrication
	Confirm Program & Space Validation	Program and Space Validation via automatic Room Data Sheets	Program and Space Validation via automatic Room Data Sheets	Program and Space Validation via automatic Room Data Sheets	Program and Space Finalised via automatic Room Data Sheets		Final room data and FF&E validated and imported into Computer-aided FM
	Initial Interference Report	Initial Interference Report	Discipline Interference Reports	Pre-Bid Interference Reports		Collision Reports	
	Comparative Square Foot Cost Estimate	Early Square Foot Cost Estimate for Selected Concept	Detailed Square Foot Cost Estimate for Selected Scheme	Elemental Cost Plan established	Bill of Quantities	BIM-based cost analysis at valuation meetings	Final cost out-turn compared to Cost Plan.
	Sustainability Analysis; Conceptual Design Analysis & Projected Energy Costs for Alternatives	Scheme Design Energy Analysis; Projected Energy Cost Report for Selected Scheme	Initial Baseline Energy Model & Analysis; Projected Energy Cost Estimate	Developed Energy Analysis against specifications and actual building/site particulars	Final Baseline Energy Model & Analysis; Finalised Energy Cost Estimate		'In-use' Energy Model mapping sub-metered usage data onto the finalised room database
	Comparative area schedules in required Information Exchange (IE) format for Facilities Management (FM)	Selected concept area schedules in required IE format for Facilities Management (FM)	Preliminary FF&E schedules in required IE format for Facilities Management (FM)	Detailed FF&E schedules in required IE format for Facilities Management (FM)	Finalised FF&E schedules in required IE format for Facilities Management (FM)	Operations Planning & Beneficial Occupancy Data in required IE format for Facilities Management (FM)	As-built Data imported to FM system (with O+M document links)

Table 2.3 The key deliverables derived from BIM for each project stage

d) The process for incorporating as-constructed, testing, validation and commissioning information.

Note that once the contract is signed, for c) and d), the BIM Manager will need to complete Appendix 2 of the CIC BIM Protocol in agreement with the EIRs. This is in order to summarise the proposed Standard Method and Procedure. In particular, the summary should outline the following:

- Applicable BIM Standard
- Common Data Environment
- Spatial Co-ordination protocol
- Model approval/information exchange protocol
- Archiving procedures
- Security requirements and access rights procedures

- Resolution of conflicts
- Process for incorporating hand-over asset information, such as commissioning data.

Appendix 1 of the CIC's *BIM Protocol* provides a tabular means of outlining items a) and b): For an explanation of the Level of detail/information for each project stage, please see Chapter 9.

PAS-1192 MODEL FEDERATION

For BIM Level 2, each project member is responsible for organising their models and associated data in separate files that reflect the scope of their responsibilities within the overall project. At regular intervals, there is a need to coordinate these in a software environment that allows their data to be combined and used as if they were a single model. It is important to note that each discipline's model can still function independently of others and will retain specific types of data that are not shared.

Model federation simply provides a common basis for combining, interrogating and interacting with exported models that contain information shared in accordance with agreed project collaboration requirements.

Table 2.4 reflects how model development responsibilities should be distributed among the various team members as work progresses. Further information on fig 9.1.

The extent of federation is important in relation to intellectual property. For instance, an engineer would not want to share a complex proprietary algorithm that is embedded in the structural model and that could leverage the data from any architect's model in order to calculate the stresses, strains and bending moments. Also, consider a library of healthcare equipment that has been customised for 1:50 room layouts and room data sheets and that contains parameters capable of producing a procurement-ready Equipment Responsibility Matrix directly from the model. Clearly, in both these cases, it would make no sense to hand over data from any model that could be used by others to replicate value-adding business

	Drop 1 Stage 1 Model Originator	Drop 2a Stage 2 Model Originator	Drop 2b Stage 2 Model Originator	Drop 3 Stage 3 Model Originator	Drop 4 Stage 6 Model Originator
Overall form and content					
Space planning	Architect	Architect	Contractor	Contractor	Contractor
Site and context	Architect	Architect	Contractor	Contractor	Contractor
Surveys			Contractor		
External form and appearance		Architect	Contractor	Contractor	Contractor
Building and site sections			Contractor	Contractor	Contractor
Internal layouts			Contractor	Contractor	Contractor
Design strategies					
Fire		Architect	Contractor	Contractor	Contractor
Physical security		Architect	Contractor	Contractor	Contractor
Disabled access		Architect	Contractor	Contractor	Contractor
Maintenance access		Architect	Contractor	Contractor	Contractor
BREEAM			Contractor	Contractor	Contractor
Performance					
Building	Architect	Architect	Contractor	Contractor	
Structural	Architect	Str Eng	Contractor	Contractor	
MEP systems	Architect	MEP Eng	Contractor	Contractor	
Regulation compliance analysis				Contractor	Contractor
Thermal Simulation				Contractor	Contractor
Sustainability Analysis				Contractor	Contractor
Acoustic analysis				Contractor	Contractor
4D Programming Analysis					
5D Cost Analysis					
Services Commissioning				Contractor	Contractor
Elements, materials components					
Building		Architect	Contractor	Contractor	Contractor
Specifications		MEP Eng	Contractor	Contractor	Contractor
MEP systems			Contractor	Contractor	Contractor
Construction proposals					
Phasing				Contractor	
Site access				Contractor	
Site set-up				Contractor	
Health and safety					
Design				Contractor	
Construction				Contractor	
Operation				Contractor	Contractor

Table 2.4 The BIM Protocol's Model Production and Delivery Table[8]

processes or hard-won efficiencies. Federation as described in the CIC BIM Protocol is an arrangement for sharing only as much of the model as is needed for the purposes permitted in the agreement. In the above engineering example, it means that the algorithm (and any parameters associated with it) can be stripped out of the model before issuing it to others via the project-wide data repository known as the Common Data Environment.

In the healthcare example, the architectural design model would be divided into a series of linked sub-models. While other sub-models could be shared in the format in which they were authored, the equipment sub-model might only be issued as either dumb geometry or in a format that does not facilitate the extraction of detailed product data.

THE BIM TOOLKIT®: DEFINING THE DELIVERABLES

The BIM Toolkit® is a portal that verifies BIM data against defined standards for modelling and embedded information. This on-line tool provides a ready means of facilitating the Information Manager's responsibilities and is a considerable advancement on tabular methods.

It provides a free-to-use set of tools to assist with the definition, management and responsibility for information development and delivery across the project lifecycle. It also confirms a classification system (Uniclass 2015) together with Level of Detail (LoD) and Level of Information (LoI) standards aligned to the RIBA / CIC / PAS1192 work stages, all supported by verification tools to confirm model compliance against predetermined project deliverables.

The functionality offered within the Toolkit delivers an effective project management tool, allowing project roles and tasks to be assigned to create a prescribed set of BIM deliverables for each project participant against each work stage. This is supported by LoD and LoI definitions provided on the website, giving greater clarity to project teams on required outputs as modelling progresses.

In practical terms, the entire team needs to decide on how best to divide the development of BIM into several models across the project (also known as the Volume Strategy) see fig. 2.4 below and then agree on a schedule for sharing updates to each model via the Common Data Environment.

What is the Project Information Model?

In PAS-1192-2, the Project Information Model is a logically organised data structure that is defined as consisting of:

- Documentation (i.e. information preserved as records of the briefing, design, construction, operation, maintenance or decommissioning of a construction project, including but not limited to correspondence, drawings, schedules, specifications, calculations, spreadsheets)

- Graphical information (i.e. data conveyed using shapes and 3D solids)

- Non-graphical information (i.e. data conveyed using text and numbers).

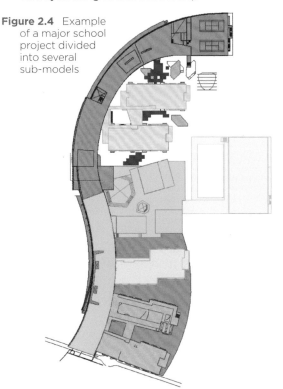

Figure 2.4 Example of a major school project divided into several sub-models

It further explains that the project information model (PIM) *'is developed firstly as a design intent model, showing the architectural and engineering intentions of the design suppliers. Then the PIM is developed into a virtual construction model containing all the objects to be manufactured, installed or constructed. It becomes the basis of the Asset Information Model once handed over.'*

In practice, the virtual construction model should be developed by the construction supply chain as a full replacement of the design intent model. In response to this requirement, the task of BIM management is to outline the plan for not only organising the variety of actionable data from all project participants into a logical structure, but also

for matching and linking that information to 3D elements which will increase in detail as the project progresses.

One image taken from PAS-1192-2 indicates the potential complexity of this task:

In the highlighted area, note how the design lead and contractor lead are expected to organise their respective sub-consultants and specialists in order to provide models to a level of detail and integrated with information upon which decisions can be made at each project stage. The management of BIM must provide and implement processes for facilitating the development and integration of project data with models from all project participants, including those at lower supply-chain tiers

Figure 2.5 PAS-1192-2 – The whole supply chain contributes information to answer the Plain Language Questions[4]

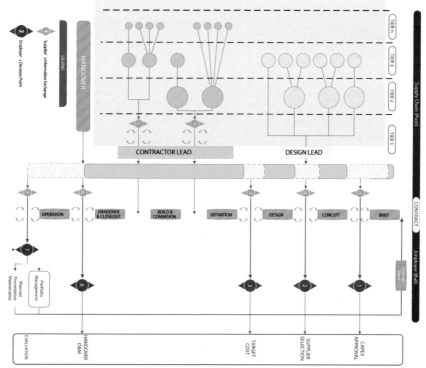

.

who are not currently *au fait* with BIM. This is probably the most challenging part of the BIM management role, and will be explained in further detail in Chapter 8.

THE FEDERATED MODEL

Both PAS-1192-2 and CIC BIM Protocol refer repeatedly to the federated model, whereby each model contribution can be developed separately and then integrated by superimposing models in a 3D software environment after exporting to the agreed file format for design review (see Chapter 10).

INTEROPERABILITY OF MODELS

It is important to note that there is nothing in these documents that mandates integrating models in the application that was used to create them. For BIM level 2, each participant can create models in proprietary software. Nevertheless, it is often better to agree on a common non-proprietary file format for reviewing and querying models in conjunction with each other. One such format is the data structure known as Industry Foundation Classes, or IFC.

In order to facilitate integration, the Standard Method and Procedure should specify a common origin and orientation for all shared models.

SUMMARY

In summary, the Pre-Contract BEP should contain:

- Roles and Responsibilities for development of the integrated model and information delivered from it throughout the project
- Summary of the proposed Common Data Environment for sharing and integrating models with associated project information
- Completed BIM, IT and resource assessment forms
- Model Production and Delivery Table
- Proposed BIM Standard and procedures for managing spatial coordination, clash resolution, model approval/information. exchange, data archival and security requirements.

THE POST-CONTRACT BIM EXECUTION PLAN

Once proposals have been accepted and the supplier approved, they are developed into the project's BIM Protocol and the more detailed Post-Contract BIM Execution Plan as a confirmation the supply chain's capabilities. The person in the role of managing BIM on behalf of the design or construction lead needs to ensure that this document is distributed to all project team members and that they have agreed and committed to this version of the BEP.

SPECIFICS TO BE CONFIRMED IN POST-CONTRACT BEP INCLUDE:

- Personnel appointed to roles, responsibilities and authorities
- Agreed matrix of responsibilities across the supply chain (see table below)
- Completed forms confirming the supply chain's capability for BIM and information Delivery.

It is worth noting that the adjective 'native', is often used in this table and elsewhere to describe any models that are issued in the original file format of the applications that generate them.

COMMON DATA ENVIRONMENT

- Volume Strategy: How will the overall project be segmented into models representing specific disciplines, zones and phases? What is the common origin point and site orientation relative to True North for all models?
- File naming convention; Layer naming convention, where used; Information approval and PIM authorisation process
- Model Production and Delivery Table: Responsibility for element categories and their development to the required level of detail at each project stage (in line with contract and the project programme)
- IT: Agreed project-wide data repository and mechanism for file sharing and notification, process and data management systems; approved software platforms; approved information exchange formats.

- Approved drawing sheet sizes, scales and templates
- Agreed units and construction tolerances for all disciplines.

INFORMATION MANAGEMENT

- Required element attributes for each project stage
- Agreed project processes/schedule for collaboration and information modelling
- Information Delivery Plans (Master and Task-level). This is an extended version of the projected sheet list; beyond drawings, it names all information deliverables that are formally required of each discipline.

SURVEY STRATEGY

- The use of point clouds, light detecting and ranging (LIDAR) or global navigation satellite systems (GNSS); use of legacy data, e.g. existing CAD drawings.

INFORMATION DELIVERY PLANS

Information delivery plans form a key part of the Post-Contract BEP. The Task Information Delivery Plans (TIDPs) are submitted by information managers from all sub-disciplines into an overall Master Information Delivery Plan (MIDP). In basic terms, the role of information manager could be assumed by each firm's document controller. The key

MODEL AUTHORING	EXAMPLE SOFTWARE	NATIVE FORMAT	EXCHANGE FORMAT(S)	PLAN OF WORK						
				1 PREPARATION AND BRIEF	2 CONCEPT DESIGN	3 DEVELOPED DESIGN	4 TECHNICAL DESIGN	5 CONSTRUCTION	6 HANDOVER AND CLOSE-OUT	7 IN USE
Space Planning										
Site, Urban Design Context										
Site and Existing Buildings										
Architectural Model										
Structural Design Model										
HVAC Design Model										
Public Health Design Model										
Lighting Design Model										
Hydraulics Design Model										
Interior Layouts and Design Model										
HVAC Fabrication Model										
Structural Steel Fabrication Model										

Table 2.5 Matrix of model authoring (creation and development) responsibilities

difference is that the responsibility for issuing correctly formatted data extends beyond hard-copy output to include a far wider variety of updateable files, including models.

PAS-1192:2 (7.4.3 to 7.4.5) explains the uses of TIDPs as follows:

- Milestones within each TIDP shall be aligned with the design and construction programmes to produce the MIDP
- For each deliverable, TIDPs shall be used to indicate the team member responsible or to note that responsibility has yet to be allocated
- TIDPs shall be used to show how responsibility for the preparation of project documents transfers from one team member to another
- TIDPs shall be used to take account of the required sequence of model preparation for any work packages used in the project.

The table below shows an example of the TIDP. The Project Architect would develop this schedule in conjunction with any other required deliverables. It is important to remember that as part of the 'Pull' strategy, the designer lead and contractor lead are expected to coordinate the lower-tier TIDPs into the Master Information Delivery Plan:

INFORMATION MANAGER

The CIC BIM Protocol outlines the Information Management role, appointed initially by the Employer. This person is therefore a client representative.

The job involves managing the following processes and procedures for information exchange on projects:

- Initiating and implementing the Project Information Plan and Asset Information Plan, including:
  - Common information structure across all project roles, e.g. non-proprietary software platforms (all levels of supply chain) appropriate to meet Employer requirements and Project Team resources
  - Responsibility for provision of information at each Project Stage
  - Establishing Level of information required for outputs at specific project stages by updating the Model Production and Delivery Table
  - The process for incorporating 'as constructed', testing, validation and commissioning information.
- Agreeing formats for Project Outputs, such as data drops
- Assisting Project Team Members in assembling information for Project Outputs
- This role does not involve clash detection and model coordination, since these are BIM Coordinator activities.

BIM managers will be expected to work closely with the client's Information Manager in order to deliver data in accordance with the agreed Employer's Information Requirements.

FILE IDENTIFIER							MODEL / DRAWING TITLE	DELIVERY DATES				
Project	Originator	Volume	Level	File type	Discipline	No		Milestone 1	Milestone 2	Milestone 3	Milestone 4	Etc.

Table 2.6 The Task Information Delivery Plan (TIDP) provides a schedule of delivery dates for formal file-based information exchange

PLAIN LANGUAGE QUESTIONS – MODEL ANSWERS

As part of the review process conducted at the end of each work stage, the client will require information from the design and construction team that will assist in project evaluation.

For each of these reviews – known as gateways – and as a means of ensuring value for money for stakeholders, plain language questions (PLQs) are used to elicit the supplier's response to the client's key criteria for authorising the project to proceed to the next stage.

PAS-1192-2 describes information exchanges as the required response to these PLQs. The information exchanges (also known as 'data drops') supply comprehensive and consistently structured data that has been collated and exported from BIM at these key project intervals.

The table on the next page is adapted from the PLQs used by the Ministry of Justice on 'early adopter' BIM projects. The second column describes data drop components formulated by the design team from the federated Project Information Model.

In describing these data drop components above, you will notice that the words 'linked' and 'exported' are used repeatedly. In each case, we are seeking through BIM to ensure that the data is being re-used, rather than incurring the expense of it being re-created.

DISTINCTIONS BETWEEN ROLES AND OFFICIAL APPOINTMENTS

While PAS-1192 and other official documents mention a number of key BIM roles, none of these is necessarily a formal full-time appointment. The scale and complexity of the project and its information requirements will determine whether the latter is justified.

For the sake of clarity, the BIM Manager is responsible for developing appropriate firm-wide BIM standards and is also the 'catalyst' who ensures that they are adopted and implemented across the entire organisation. The next chapter will show how the BIM Manager's role can be developed by encouraging and training an existing staff member to become the initial BIM champion. Nevertheless, there is the caveat that extending a role in this way indefinitely without an official appointment or adequate remuneration may be counter-productive, especially if it leads to eventual disillusionment and the BIM champion's decision to take their acquired BIM skills elsewhere.

The role of Information Manager is project-focused and akin to that of a document controller. The distinction lies in the wide variety of data that must be vetted by the Information Manager for issue at each project milestone. This extends far beyond static hard-copy documentation to include the full range of model types that must be collected, combined and exported with other data for information, visualisation and analysis purposes.

The BIM coordinator is a project role, normally assigned to a design or construction professional on the team. This person is instrumental in reducing the likelihood of inter-disciplinary design and construction conflicts by working under the guidance of the technical coordinator in order to resolve coordination issues in the 3D model environment (as described in Chapter 5).

PLAIN LANGUAGE QUESTIONS	BIM LEVEL 2 DATA DROP COMPONENTS
How have stakeholder requirements from the workshop process been captured and addressed?	Report from database linked to model and capturing all requirements from stakeholder workshops. Briefing data also used for comparison with documented design intent, i.e. drawings, schedules, analysis output and visualisations exported from the model:
Does the requirement developed to date meet the stakeholder's needs?	Database linked to model used to export requirements as equipment schedules, room data sheets. Checked against layout drawings exported from BIM with corresponding FF&E and room tags.
What are the physical constraints around the site?	Integration of existing BIM/GIS survey, or commissioned laser survey with 3D conceptual model.
What is the view of capital cost at this time?	Schedules of gross internal floor area by level and development areas and volumes derived from 3D conceptual models. Key ratios calculated. Data checked and exported into elemental cost analysis format with the addition of cost data by cost planner.
What is the outline proposal for structural design?	Structural model coordinated with architecture sufficient for loads simulation. Size and weight information imported in model. Temporary construction loads analysed in model.
What is the services strategy?	Schematic drawings; layout drawings and models coordinating supply utility locations, plant rooms, risers, and 'first-pass' primary services routes; preliminary plant room layouts. Colour coded system zones and schedules of room loads data imported into model to demonstrate services sufficient for early iterations of spatial requirements.
Progress on BREEAM (Building Research Establishment Environmental Assessment Method) compliance, including any issues that have arisen.	Analysis of exported low-detail 3D environmental room data model (in gbXML format) to generate BREEAM compliance reports.
What is the impact of the proposals on surrounding buildings?	Multiple 3D renderings, solar studies of early concepts in context of modelled surrounding.

Table 2.7 Plain Language Questions and BIM 'data drop' responses[5]

CONCLUSION

The Government Construction Strategy, and the guidance of PAS-1192-2 in particular, has established BIM Level 2 as the benchmark framework for implementing a regime of exchanging information via data linked to elements comprising the issued 3D model. BIM Level 2 involves the design lead and/or contractor lead marshalling their respective supply chains to deliver critical project data which represents the key inputs of all specialists and sub-contractors in conjunction with their combined models.

In the absence of in-house expertise, the client should rely upon an experienced external technical adviser to formulate the Employer's Information Requirements for this type of project delivery via BIM.

As a rule, it is important to conduct a careful assessment of the Employer's Information Requirements, requesting clarification and amendment where necessary. In response to these requirements, the design and construction suppl zier are expected to develop coherent pre- and post-contract iterations of the BIM Project Execution Plan.

The Information Manager is appointed initially by the Employer to ensure that timely information is provided in the correct format and to the correct level of detail, in accordance with:

• The Model Production and Delivery Table
• Task/Master Information Delivery Plans
• BIM Protocol.

[1] BIM Working Party strategy paper, 2011 Department of Business, Innovation and Skills: United Kingdom, p.16.
[2] ibid. p.37
[3] ibid. p.3
[4] PAS 1192-2:2013, Specification for information management for the capital/delivery phase of construction projects using building information modelling, 2013: British Standards Institution.
[5] BIM Task Group, BIM Employer's Information Requirements (EIR) Core Content and Guidance, 2013 <http://www.bimtaskgroup.org/wp-content/uploads/2013/04/Employers-Information-Requirements-Core-Content-and-Guidance.pdf>, p.1.
[6] RIBA Plan of Work 2013 <http://www.ribaplanofwork.com/>
[7] Outline Scope of Services for the Role of information Management, 2013: Construction Industry Council.
[8] CIC BIM Protocol, 2013, Construction Industry Council

03

ASSESSING YOUR PRACTICE
AND GUIDING IT TO
BIM-READINESS

INTRODUCTION

We begin this chapter by identifying the three characteristics that are key to the successful implementation of BIM. In particular, it is recommended that firms adopt a gradual tiered approach. This progresses in stages, from first deploying BIM to improve the basic cost of doing business, to eventual 'next frontier' BIM investments.

The key coverage of this chapter is as follows;
* The three characteristics of BIM implementation success
* Tiered investment in BIM for design, construction and operations
* Precursors to BIM Level 2 project delivery
* Assessing your firm's BIM readiness
* Organisational BIM assessment.

THE THREE CHARACTERISTICS OF BIM IMPLEMENTATION SUCCESS

For the implementation of BIM to deliver measurable success, there is considerable evidence[1] that managerial innovation must develop in conjunction with technology to facilitate the following kinds of beneficial change:

* More effective deployment of the firm's workforce
* Increasing the efficiency of staff in delivering the current range of services
* The development of new services that clients perceive as adding value.

A tiered approach to implementing BIM provides time for managerial innovation to keep up with the pace of technology adoption.

TIERED INVESTMENT IN BIM FOR DESIGN, CONSTRUCTION AND OPERATIONS

The table on the facing page, consisting of four progressive tiers, provides a way of assessing your firm's current position on the BIM maturity ladder. It also indicates that the technology for each tier should be implemented comprehensively as a precursor to success at the next level.

For instance, if a project team lacks documented in-house design publishing standards (BIM Level 0) or has no experience or success in establishing a Common Data Environment for collaboration through CAD (BIM Level 1), they are unlikely to achieve the benefits of coordinated information exchange through BIM at Level 2.

Equally, it makes no sense for a construction supply chain team to make the bold transition to a server-based Integrated Building Model environment (BIM Level 3) when its attempts to regularly coordinate independently generated models at BIM Level 2 have foundered badly.

The above is not to say that organisations must meticulously introduce every element of BIM Levels 0 and 1 adoption before implementing BIM Level 2. Nevertheless, they must attend to the features of Levels 0 and 1 that are foundational to Level 2.

Figure 3.1 Tiers of BIM investment from CAD-based collaboration to fully integrated BIM[1]

BIM FOR BASIC COST OF BUSINESS	BIM FOR EXTENDED COST OF BUSINESS	'DIFFERENTIATING' BIM INVESTMENTS	'NEXT FRONTIER' BIM INVESTMENTS
			▶ BIM Level 3 – 'Real-time' querying of comprehensive model integrated with supply chain operations and actual built environment
		▶ BIM Level 2 – Semi-automated design/construction coordination in 3D, production and asset information	Solutions that enhance client experience: e.g. 'self-service' decision-support environments; post-occupancy asset data and building performance monitoring (PAS-1192-5)
	▶ BIM Level 1 – Visual 2D/3D coordination of multi-disciplinary production information	Marketable supply chain innovations in Design/Construction Process Integration and in Building Performance Improvement	
▶ BIM Level 0	Protocols implemented to manage exchange and coordination of project data for supply chain efficiency (BS-1192:2007)	Federation: agreement on integration platform for coordinating multiple 3D BIM inputs from different applications. (PAS-1192-2, 4; BS-1192-3)	Client review and approval via 'self-service' interrogation of server-based Integrated Building Model using IFC as common format
Static 2D Design Deliverables (paper, PDF) Documented design publication standards and templates	Managed 2D/3D Design Libraries (BS-8541-1, 2) and Common Data Environment- 'used to collect, manage and disseminate all relevant approved project documents for multi-disciplinary teams	Managed data-enriched 3D Design Libraries (BS-8541-3, 4)	→
Firm-wide Resource/Work Planning and Financial/HR Management Systems	Project Data Management Systems. Shared Design/Construction Issue Tracking Systems		→
Core Solutions supporting In-house Operations: CAD, Office Productivity (e.g. word processing, spreadsheet) and Project Management applications	CAD Management Systems (layers, file/folder naming) to enforce common protocols for differentiating contributions from each project participant (BS-1192:2007)		→
NETWORKING, DATABASE AND SECURITY INFRASTRUCTURE INVESTMENT			

PRECURSORS TO BIM LEVEL 2 PROJECT DELIVERY

Nevertheless, for the delivery of projects at BIM Level 2, it is essential to establish some aspects of those lower tiers:

- Leadership roles in firms that are new to BIM
- Documented design publication standards
- Project data management and issue tracking systems
- Management of data-rich model content
- Usage of a data storage naming protocol
- Standardised file-based design coordination processes.

Leadership roles in firms that are new to BIM

Whether your firm is a conglomerate or a small design practice, there are two preparatory roles that are indispensable to the success of a firm's BIM adoption. These are the *BIM Sponsor* and the *BIM Champion* and they should precede even formally established BIM Manager and BIM Coordinator roles. (The role of BIM Manager is explained in the section of Chapter 2 entitled **Distinctions between roles and official appointments.**)

Despite the importance of adherence to BIM standards, for small to medium enterprises (SMEs), there remains justifiable concern about hiring BIM staff in advance of winning a project that requires Level 2 compliance. For these companies, it is important to emphasise that the PAS-1192 specifies leadership roles, and not full-time appointments for BIM. The BIM Sponsor should be a senior officer of the firm who will exercise strategic influence in setting corporate goals and objectives for BIM adoption. This role requires direct authority over major resources. In contrast, the BIM Champion could be much further down the organisational chain of command, but be a person who has shown the ability to gain the support of colleagues in implementing technological change.

What sort of influence is needed to implement BIM successfully?

In *Influence: The Psychology of Persuasion.*[2] Robert Cialdini identified six key factors that were employed in influencing and persuading others to adopt a course of action. These are:

- Authority: People will tend to obey those bestowed with firm-wide authority
- Commitment and Consistency: People do not like to be self-contradictory. Once they commit to an idea or behaviour, they are averse to changing their minds without good reason
- Liking: People are more easily persuaded by people they like
- Reciprocity: People have a sense of obligation to return a favour
- Social Proof: People tend to conform to the consensus of the majority
- Scarcity: A perceived sense of BIM as a prioritised opportunity for advancement will fuel interest.

This means that the firm-wide implementation of BIM, which involves major organisational change, cannot be effected by authority and expertise alone. It also requires leadership. The latter can be exercised by any person who has the support and social skills needed to enlist other staff in the task of company transformation. It is important to note that while the roles needed to implement BIM Level 2 should eventually be invested with official authority, the organisation should begin by identifying those members of staff who have demonstrable social and leadership skills. While many practices view an IT specialist or an enthusiastic design technologist as the obvious choice to become BIM Champion, there are other less technically adept but nonetheless persistent and charismatic individuals who might be more effective.

On that basis, here are seven recommendations that will help the prospective BIM Sponsor and Champion to lead successfully.

1   Ensure you communicate clear, positive and consistent messages to the team about the business improvement vision and mission for using BIM.

2   Provide a carefully paced schedule for gradually deploying BIM over three or four years across all project sectors without overstretching (and thereby disillusioning) the project teams. For instance, in year one, you could begin by creating large-scale general arrangement drawings from the 3D model to scheme design stage for a number of projects in a couple of sectors, such as residential and commercial. By year three, the firm could then expand to healthcare and education, where the requirements for deliverables can be far more prescriptive. At the same time, the practice could start to develop more detailed schedules and drawing types from the model.

3   Don't restrict the scope for deploying BIM to a few types of projects.

4   Don't restrict the use of BIM to projects for which the client requests it.

5   Support employee development with time for formal BIM training and staff mentoring. Given the initial lack of knowledge, design practices and construction firms are usually willing to pay for staff to attend fundamentals training on BIM software. At that level of training, end-users will gain a 'hands-on' understanding of the creation and organisation of basic 3D and 2D elements, views, annotations and sheets.

6   As a minimum, provide office-wide recognition as a reward for BIM champions who successfully implement planned initiatives; better still, develop incentives that are linked to process improvement objectives.

7   Provide a regular forum for staff to participate in identifying and resolving unforeseen teething problems and in refining processes for producing high-quality deliverables from the new software.

Tackling the effect of late BIM adoption on leadership priorities

'Crossing the Chasm' is a best-selling management guide written by technology adoption expert Dr Geoffrey A. Moore. In it, Moore explains that in fact there is a discontinuity, known as the chasm, which hinders the mainstream adoption of innovations, like BIM.[3]

While it is relatively easy for firms to adopt technologies that simply improve on the existing mechanisms by which they add value – these are known as sustaining technologies and are represented by exactly what CAD did for 2D manual drafting – a disruptive innovation like BIM will, by contrast, immediately emphasise tools that the mainstream considers secondary to its core business. These tools may lack some of the features that are important to the prevailing use of computer graphics technology (CAD). The genuine (and partly justified) concern of the sceptical is that, whatever the claimed benefits, the new technology will incur significant additional costs due to new software, customised configurations, additional staff training, specialised support personnel and structured implementation programmes.

The unexpected tipping point for these firms to implement the new technology is when the capabilities of the latter (for example, 3D coordination and automatic schedules) are suddenly prioritised by clients. As more and more Requests for Proposals seek detailed evidence of documented processes for reducing design re-work through features such as multi-disciplinary clash detection, it may indeed prompt a thorough investigation of BIM adoption across the competitive landscape. Nevertheless, the way to catch up should not involve the knee-jerk reaction of recruiting a BIM Manager immediately and trying to source a requisite 'box' of BIM.

In a 2013 study by Eadie et al, 'An Analysis of the Drivers for Adopting BIM' (*ITcon* Vol. 18 (2013))[4], current users and non-users of BIM were contrasted in terms of the relative importance they placed on different drivers for implementing the technology:

From the graph, it's important to notice that the drivers for current non-BIM users are primarily Government Pressure, Client Pressure and Competitive Pressure. The mooted benefits of BIM are secondary factors for those who have not yet deployed the technology.

In an organisation that is only just beginning to think about adopting BIM, the role of a BIM Sponsor would probably be that of a boardroom pioneer, venturing forth into uncharted territory with a mandate focused more on alleviating these competitive

pressures, rather than on the full integration of BIM into current work practices.

This is important because, if BIM adoption is solely driven by competitive pressures, it will not be viewed in terms of delivering process improvement. Instead, it will be jettisoned when other initiatives require major investment and are considered more capable of impressing potential clients.

In those circumstances, it will be difficult for a BIM sponsor to gain the level of adoption needed to make a success of BIM. What is needed in this situation is for the board to review case studies, to talk to firms that are further along in BIM adoption, and to devise a long-term strategy (see Chapter 1) for achieving all three characteristics of BIM success, while remaining aligned with the asset management strategy of its clients.

Figure 3.2 Relative importance of BIM adoption drivers to current BIM users and non-users[4]

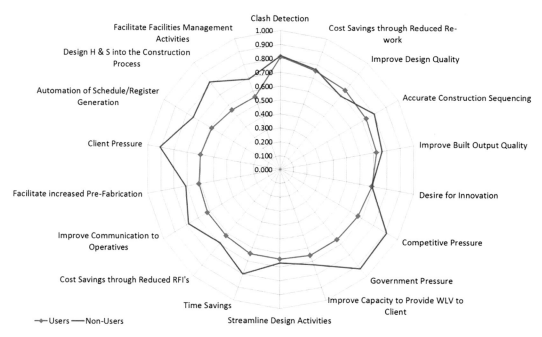

ESTABLISH DOCUMENTED DESIGN PUBLICATION STANDARDS

Project documentation should – like other organisational publications – maintain a consistent corporate identity. Consistency conveys positive messages about service reliability and professionalism. Establishing a 'house style' for conventionally required project deliverables is the most basic level of output consistency.

If a practice cannot maintain and manage consistency for even its published design documentation, it will be impossible to control the quality of additional data derived from BIM and exchanged in digital format. Documentation and training should be provided to establish the firm's default publication standards for the full variety of typical drawing types and scales. Provision for project-specific variations to these standards should be documented in the BIM Project Execution Plan (described in Chapter 2).

This process of adopting publication standards is facilitated by the provision of drawing border templates, an approved symbol library and especially by approved exemplar drawings.

It's worth noting that on completing the fundamentals training course, the users will able to repeat the steps that they followed, but will not be able to apply them immediately, confidently and quickly to a variety of project types. It will take a few months of post-training practice for these skills to develop sufficiently for them to complete a basic small-scale scheme design submission via BIM. Even after this, there are further skills specific to more challenging project work in BIM that will, once mastered, deliver benefits across the entire practice.

In weighing these benefits against the marginal implementation of the technology, it would make sense to budget for more advanced training for staff to accomplish the following:

- Over the course of the project, the ability to create, control and refine model elements

with more realistic levels of detail and information than the standard libraries provided with the software.

- For larger schemes, the ability to generate design deliverables from a series of smaller inter-linked models and views.
- The ability to apply sophisticated templates to multiple model views and sheets for consistent publication-quality output.
- Reduction in the use of superimposed 2D drafting by developing model elements that display their conventional CAD representations in plan, section and elevation views.

PROJECT DATA MANAGEMENT AND ISSUE TRACKING SYSTEMS

Let's assume that, in line with the Government Construction Strategy, a firm has agreed on the following BIM goals:

- Reduction/elimination of coordination errors
- Improved ease in using the model to compare alternative design/ construction proposals.

Whereas the former provides the benefit of better integrated multi-disciplinary design and construction information, the latter ensures that the client can identify the salient differences between several design alternatives with greater speed and clarity. Within the project data management system, it is possible to compare the threads of discussion associated with a variety of coordination issues and design options before and after implementing BIM. The tracking system should be reviewed regularly to compare the relative length and content of email exchanges for similar issues relating to projects of similar complexity. This should provide both qualitative and quantitative comparisons of whether BIM has reduced coordination errors and improved the ease with which clients review design alternatives.

In fact, there is little hope of evaluating these improvements objectively without a system for managing project data and tracking design and contractor issues through to resolution.

While the IT systems developed for these purposes can range from simple email add-ons to dedicated full-featured applications, none can function effectively without full staff cooperation. This is best accomplished by setting expectations through documented standards, providing support, encouragement and training at all levels and ensuring that the board of management endorses and adheres to these firm-wide standards as central (rather than peripheral) to its strategic goals.

Firms that engage in partnering will need to adopt project-wide protocols and data management in order to ensure that data and issue tracking is managed consistently across the various disciplines involved in the process of delivery.

MANAGEMENT OF DATA-RICH MODEL CONTENT

In addition to documented templates and output standards, responsibility for managing the quality of project deliverables should be clearly assigned. Initially, this would be the task of the organisation's BIM Champion – the chief librarian of model content. Their main task is to organise model elements (which should be consistent in the level of detail and information) into a logical folder structure. The file names and the specification data attached to them should be sufficient to facilitate efficient library searches. This measure is efficient since the time taken for one person to archive the elements regularly from each project into a shared office-wide library is easily recouped through their subsequent re-use (vs. re-creation) by the teams assigned to future projects.

Library objects are graphic representations of design/construction components that are classified by attaching data to them to define their 'real world' properties.

The image on the left shows a library object from the online **NBS National BIM Library** as defined for a particular floor type. The NBS BIM Object Standard - **http://www.nationalbimlibrary. com/nbs-bim-object-standard**. The list on the left specifies the various properties associated with the 'real world' equivalent of this floor type. These properties are also known as data attributes.

In its role as the organisation responsible for UK building specification standards, the NBS has developed a variety of other BIM objects as exemplars for those being uploaded to the same library by building product manufacturers.

Consistency in classifying and assigning the full range of data attributes enables them to be accurately and efficiently re-used throughout the project lifecycle. For instance, one of the floor attributes shown on the left has the NBS Reference 20-55-05/115, a reference to the applicable specification clause. The NBS reference uses Uniclass 2, the nationally recognised classification system for construction activities and elements and for different building operations and usages. Every building product

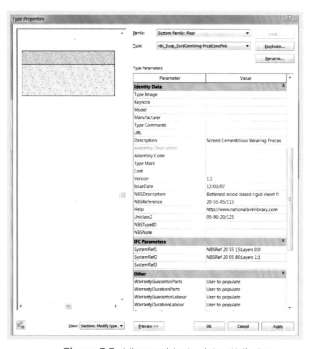

Figure 3.3   Library object - data attributes for a floor type[5]

specified through NBS should reference this classification system.

For a given project stage, if this data can relied upon in accordance with the agreed level of information (see Chapter 9), it can be developed and transferred to others through the use of the model.

For instance, by means of the NBS Create on-line specification creation tool, the specifier would create the corresponding detailed specification clauses. These clauses would be linked to instances of the same library objects in the model. On receipt of the model and the file generated by NBS Create (*.spex), the contractor's estimators would use NBS Plus (a product search tool within NBS Create) to search for products that comply with the issued specification.

By comparison with previous, slower methods of accomplishing the same task (by exchanging either paper, or spreadsheets and electronic prints), this re-use of digital specification data represents considerable time-saving. Nevertheless, this saving is squandered when someone in the process abandons compatible formats for those that limit re-use in other software applications.

Specification, assessment and simulation attributes

In fact, the different types of data attributes, in accordance with BS-8541-4, fall into three major categories described below:

- Specification attributes, as explained in the floor example above, facilitate the procurement and replacement of building elements

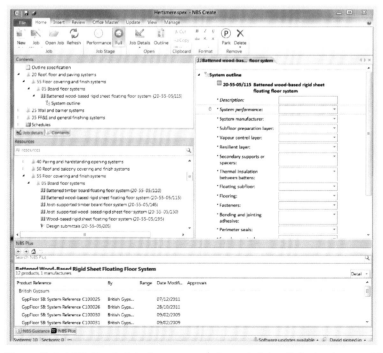

Figure 3.4 NBS Create interface re-uses element data attributes for specification[6]

- Assessment attributes facilitate economic and environmental impact assessment. An example would be the Environmental Product Declaration number, which can be correlated with an official document that verifies the resources and energy expended in the production of a particular element, as well as the resulting carbon and other emissions. See http://www.environdec.com/en/What-is-an-EPD/
- Simulation attributes facilitate performance assessment. For instance, a particular chiller would be assigned simulation attributes for Coefficient of Performance and Distribution Efficiency. The M&E sub-contractor would re-use these attributes in BIM-enabled software that can evaluate the design engineer's choice of mechanical plant.

On behalf of the project team, the BIM Manager should establish a definitive list of the key attributes (also known as parameters) that should be consistently applied to various categories of model elements. This list becomes the basis for element scheduling, comparison and sorting.

USING A DATA STORAGE NAMING PROTOCOL

An essential part of BIM-readiness is a consistent naming protocol for data storage elements such as folders, files and sub-file element groupings. This allows users to apply standardised criteria for sifting quickly through large amounts of multi-disciplinary data.

While BS-1192:2007 provides a framework for this purpose, it was primarily developed with BIM Level 1 CAD file exchange in mind.

While this may be fine for CAD file exchange, its length makes it unsuitable for annotating title blocks and drawing reference symbols, such as section and elevation marks.

For the latter, the naming of views within the model environment should be truncated and read in conjunction with the sheet name in the title block (see below).

DOCUMENT NUMBER								REVISION
Field 1	Field 2	Field 3	Field 4	Field 5	Field 6	Field 7	Field 8	Field 9
ABC	SRV	02	M3	ZZ	S	21	0001	P01
Project	Originator	Zone	Type	Level	Role	Element	Sequential Number	Revision

Figure 3.5 BS-1192 file name convention[7]

PRJ-HOK-02-M3-ZZ-A-21-0001-P01

Figure 3.6 Section Mark referencing the complete BS-1192 sheet name

A-21-0001-P01

Figure 3.7 Section Mark referencing an abbreviation of the full BS-1192 sheet name

STANDARDISING FILE-BASED DESIGN COORDINATION PROCESSES

BS-1192 outlines the recommended revision process that uses superimposed CAD drawings (known as reference files, or xrefs) for multi-disciplinary visual coordination. For instance, the engineer would ensure that the duct layout being drawn in the mechanical CAD file correctly fits the corridor layout by displaying the architect's floor plan CAD file as a background.

The name of a file issued as a subsequent revision to the previous architectural floor plan drawing would be suffixed P02 and distributed through the project's file sharing repository.

This process also works well for exchanging models. Revisions to a previously uploaded model suffixed P01 should be uploaded to the shared project repository with a suffix increment, i.e. P02.

According to BS-1192, after issuing the revision, the work-in-progress file name would be updated to P02.1 and thereafter in .1 increments until the model is shared with the suffix P03. The application of these intermediate increments before a major revision is known as *versioning.*

While this process helps to easily distinguish updates in the model made internally and externally, it can be further complicated by changes of design development responsibility at each stage of the project. So, for instance, at a certain stage, the architect may delete some elements from the model (say, architectural columns) while the engineer replaces them with their versions of those elements (structural columns).

This part of the standard should not be mandated for the internal use of BIM software that can create and store several work-in-progress versions as part of its backup functionality.

Users can also set the number of backups that will be stored in the sub-folder where the model is located.

If the maximum number of backups is set to 10, it signifies that when backup 11 is completed, the first backup will no longer be

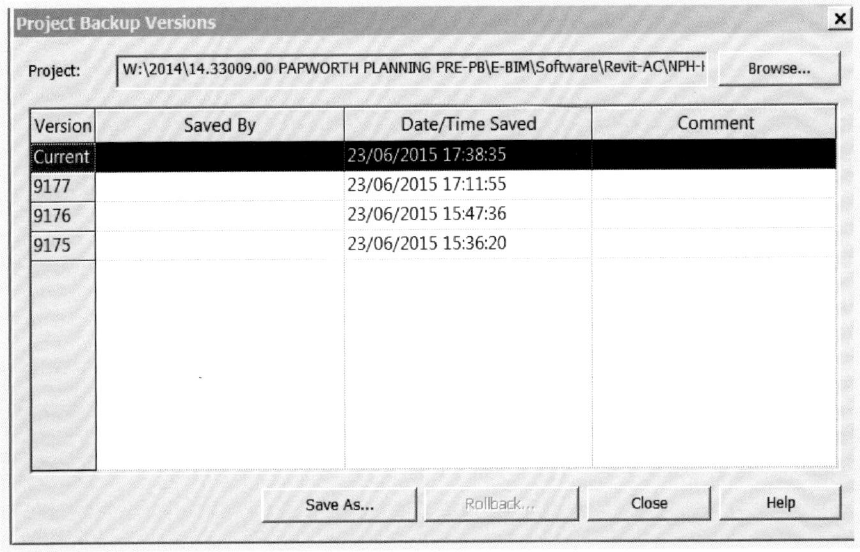
Project Backup Versions
Project:
W:\2014\14.33009.00 PAPWORTH PLANNING PRE-PB\E-BIM\Software\Revit-AC\NPH-
Browse...
Version
Saved By
Date/Time Saved
Comment
Current
23/06/2015 17:38:35
9177
23/06/2015 17:11:55
9176
23/06/2015 15:47:36
9175
23/06/2015 15:36:20
Save As...
Rollback...
Close
Help

Figure 3.8 Model backups listed in Restore dialog box (Autodesk Revit®)[5]

Figure 3.9 Dialog box option for setting number of backups to 10 (Autodesk Revit®)[5]

retrievable by this means. For this reason, the organisation's IT administrator should ensure that, for all projects, these backup subfolders are part of the daily folder system backup procedure. It's also useful to run spot checks by posing an unexpected request for IT to retrieve a particular backup folder from a particular date.

If your BIM software has this backup functionality, the recommendation for applying BS-1192 to model naming internally would be to drop the revision/version suffix:

As well as being easier to implement, this naming convention also works in alignment with the known capabilities of BIM software.

For files exchanged with external parties through the Common Data Environment, it still makes good sense to add the revision suffix as a means of distinguishing updates issued by each project team member.

Additionally, design responsibilities might need to be assigned at the level of sub-elements located in separate models. For instance, the structural floor would be modelled in the engineer's model, while its corresponding suspended floor is located in the architectural model.

In these instances, it is advisable to maintain a separate but linked model file dedicated to the sharing and monitoring of changes to datums such as gridlines, levels and reference geometry, including the building footprint and site offsets.

ORGANISATIONAL BIM ASSESSMENT

A key part of preparing for BIM Level 2 is to conduct an organisational assessment of its capabilities. The CPix BIM Assessment forms (examples at http://www.cpic.org.uk/cpix/cpix-bim-assessment-file/) are questionnaires that are now a key part of Pre-Qualification Questionnaires used to evaluate tenderers.

Making sense of every question may feel daunting for practices or construction companies that are new to BIM. Nevertheless, answering these questions with candour provides a useful self-assessment of the current readiness to implement BIM Level 2.

DOCUMENT NUMBER							
Field 1	Field 2	Field 3	Field 4	Field 5	Field 6	Field 7	Field 8
ABC	SRV	02	M3	ZZ	S	21	0001
Project	Originator	Zone	Type	Level	Role	Element	Sequential Number

Figure 3.10 Example of internal work-in-progress file naming convention

The assessment questions relate to three key concerns:

- The organisational significance of BIM.
- Resourcing and commitment to BIM for coordination and in-depth review of design alternatives.
- The organisational, office and project roles involved in driving BIM adoption.

The five sections of the assessment will need to be completed as a means of demonstrating capability to deliver projects at BIM Level 2:

- Standard Information (contact details).
- BIM 'Gateway' Questions – responses should demonstrate firm-wide commitment to project data management standards, iterative model development processes, model element libraries, training programmes, qualifications and coordination in BIM.
- Understanding and supporting evidence relating to 12 key applications of BIM.
- Minimum of three recent reference projects using BIM.
- Detailed BIM Capability Questionnaire.

While no company can gain BIM project experience overnight, assessing BIM readiness at regular intervals along the course of adoption can still be thoroughly valuable exercise.

CONCLUSION

BIM Level 2 readiness will never be achieved through short-term initiatives. This is because its efficiencies are primarily inter-departmental and inter-organisational. As such, firm-wide roles, such as the BIM Sponsor and BIM Champion, and long-term resource commitment are key to its success.

We have identified six essential precursor to BIM Level 2 readiness. By conducting a regular BIM capability assessment, you can ascertain whether they are in place.

In the next chapter, we review the expectations of the clients in terms of BIM maturity levels.

[1] How IT enables growth, 2002 McKinsey Global Institute: San Francisco
[2] R.B. Cialdini, *Influence: The Psychology of Persuasion,* 1984: US
[3] Dr. Geoffrey A. Moore, *Crossing the Chasm,* 1991, HarperBusiness: New York
[4] Eadie et al., 'An Analysis of the Drivers for Adopting BIM', 2013 *ITcon* Vol.18
[5] Autodesk screen shots reprinted with the permission of Autodesk, Inc.
[6] Courtesy of RIBA Enterprises Ltd.
[7] Copyright British Standards Institution

BIM ADOPTION AND MATURITY LEVELS

INTRODUCTION

The Department for Business Innovation and Skills (BIS) formed a Working Party in 2010 to advise the government as the construction client on national policy for the transitioning to BIM. The Working Party's BIM Strategy Paper presented the technology adoption as maturing through distinct phases, called BIM Maturity Levels. This chapter explains these levels in the practical terms of the main collaborative processes of each for an organisation. It concludes with a section on setting goals and objectives for BIM adoption.

The key coverage of this chapter is as follows;
- What does BIM maturity look like?
- Goal setting for design and construction collaboration in BIM.

WHAT DOES BIM MATURITY LOOK LIKE?

LEVELS OF DATA INTEGRATION AND COLLABORATIVE WORKING

The diagram on the facing page is attributed to Mervyn Richards and Mark Bew, both key architects of the Government BIM Strategy.

The slope represents the adoption of BIM as a trajectory of increasing collaboration through better integration of project data with computer-based graphics elements.

The maturity of this integration falls into distinct phases, or levels. These range from uncoordinated 2D drawing production using CAD (Level 0) to project and asset data

0	Unmanaged CAD, probably 2D, with paper (or electronic paper) as the most likely data exchange mechanism.
1	Managed CAD in 2D or 3D format using BS1192:2007 with a collaboration tool providing a common data environment, possibly some standard data structures and formats. Commercial data managed by standalone finance and cost management packages with no integration.
2	Managed 3D environment held in separate discipline 'BIM' tools with attached data. Commercial data managed by an ERP. Integration on the basis of proprietary interfaces or bespoke middleware could be regarded as 'pBIM' (proprietary). The approach may use 4D programme data and 5D cost elements as well as feed operational systems.
3	Fully open process and data integration enabled by 'web services' compliant with emerging IFC / IFD standards, managed by a collaborative model server. Could be regarded as iBIM or 'integrated BIM', potentially employing concurrent engineering processes.

Table 4.1 BIM maturity descriptions

mapped to elements in searchable integrated web-based 3D building models (Level 3)

In the BIM Working Party's Strategy Paper[2] (commissioned by the UK Department for Business Innovation and Skills), the BIM Maturity Levels as defined as shown on the facing page.

WORKING AT LEVEL 0

BIM Level 0 means that, although drawings are prepared in an editable CAD format, the exchange of project data is largely paper-based. This level includes the exchange of electronic paper formats, such as PDF. While these formats are readable, they are not particularly reusable for drafting purposes.

Figure 4.1 The Bew-Richards BIM maturity diagram[1]

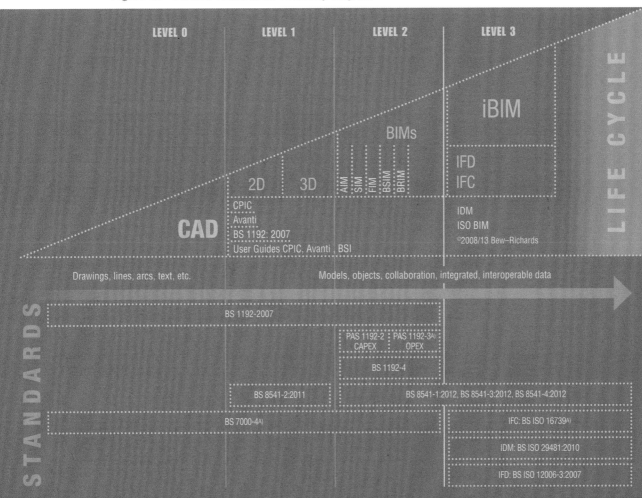

One key capability of CAD is that it allows users to organise drawing elements into distinct layers. This feature gives control over the presentation and visibility of different groups of elements.

The British Standard for coordinating project information in CAD, BS-1192:2007,[3] provides detailed guidance on how layers should be implemented to manage the exchange of drawing information. Nevertheless, if a design practice uses CAD systems to prepare its drawings, but doesn't exchange those files with other project members in accordance with a common layer naming convention, they are still operating at BIM Level 0.

In its introduction, BS-1192 mentions the challenges associated with unmanaged CAD: *'Each year considerable resources are spent on making corrections to non-standard data, training new personnel in approved data creation techniques, coordinating the efforts of subcontractor teams and solving problems related to data reproduction.'*

This observation must resonate with those practices experiencing frustration with incompatible CAD file formats and inconsistent layer and file naming.

WHAT IS LEVEL 1?

In order to address these challenges, the focus of moving from Level 0 to Level 1 is on applying a regime of standardised processes for sequentially naming, distributing and combining the distinct 2D and 3D CAD contributions of each project participant in an organised and efficient manner. The focus at Level 1 is on the production of coordinated drawings, and not on the use of any information that might be embedded or linked to them.

For BIM Level 1, the architect will initiate the project team's file-based drawing exchange process by the first issue. Typically, this would be via an online file storage portal configured for the project. An automatic notification of the upload would be issued through this portal to other participants.

The team of consultants will download, but not modify, each other's drawings. Instead, they use a key capability of CAD that allows them to utilise each discipline's drawing files as a background to their own drawings (in CAD terminology, these backgrounds are variously known as external references, or reference files).

For BIM Level 1, the project team work with a common layer structure to organise all of the drawn information that they exchange through CAD. For instance, in accordance with BS-1192, the architectural elements would be placed on layers with names prefixed by 'A'. Similarly, the structural engineer's components would be assigned to a set of layers beginning with 'S'. Beam elements would be distinguished from columns by placing them on a different layer. The process of assigning elements to various layers may even be automated by sophisticated programming routines.

At BIM Level 1, the naming convention is extended to other elements, such as folders and files. The conscientious organisation of drawings into consistently named layers, files and folders provides a ready means of searching, isolating and coordinating the various elements from each discipline.

In order to maintain consistent positioning, it is important for all drawings to share a common reference location, i.e. origin, and for them to be oriented by the same angle relative to true North. Once agreed, this shared positioning ensures that drawings can be inserted into each other without the time-consuming effort of having to adjust them repeatedly.

Central to Level 1 maturity is the establishment of a Common Data Environment. This is the collaboration tool that BS-1192 describes as 'a repository, for example a project extranet or electronic document management system' which will 'allow information to be shared between all members of the project team'. Its key capabilities are described further in Chapter 8.

WHAT IS LEVEL 2?

BIM Level 2 builds upon Level 1 and represents the next development in multi-disciplinary design/construction data integration.

For BIM Level 2:

- The BIM software used to create each model can be specific to each discipline. For example, the architects might use

Graphisoft ArchiCAD®, while structural engineers develop the beams, columns, braces and their connections in Revit Structure®. At the same time, the building services engineers might opt for AutoCAD MEP®. Although the client, lead designer or main contractor might still demand native models, there is no imperative in the British Standards documentation for the project team to exchange them in that format.

Figure 4.2 BIM Level 2: Collaboration using a federated model[4]

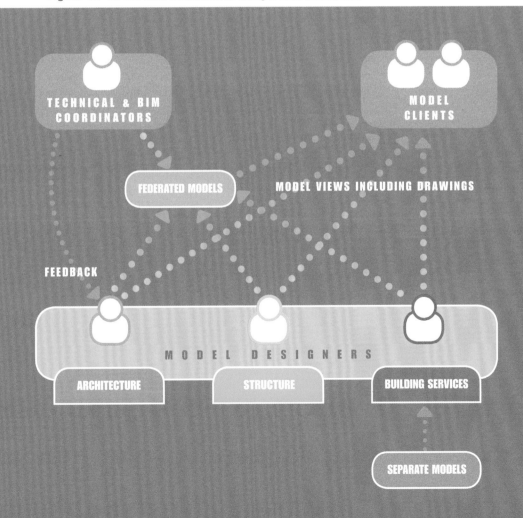

Project team members are not obliged to use the same core software application in order to create their models; instead, typically, the tools that they use to produce and update their own model files are those best suited to their respective specialties.

- The BIM Level 2 definition given in Table 4.1 refers to 'proprietary interfaces or bespoke middleware'. These terms describe another software package that acts as a bridge by combining models that might otherwise be incompatible – a process known as *model federation.* In layman's terms, agreeing on this proprietary interface means that, while the project team are free to use a variety of applications for generating models, all of them must be capable of being exported to a common format that allows them to be combined by means of the software 'bridge'.

Examples of programs that can combine models which vary in native file format include Autodesk Navisworks®, Bentley Project Navigator®, Tekla BIMSight® and Solibri Model Checker®.

Since these files will be merged into a federated model, they should be exported in a format that preserves their original geometry, the model's location in 3D space and links to any associated data. In the British Standard PAS-1192-2, these exported files are called model renditions.

- Commercial data can be managed by an enterprise resource planning system (ERP)'. ERP systems are the major applications that integrate information-based processes across the many functional departments of a large business, such as those of a main contractor.

In comparison with CAD geometry, BIM elements contain significantly more properties to which end-users can add data.

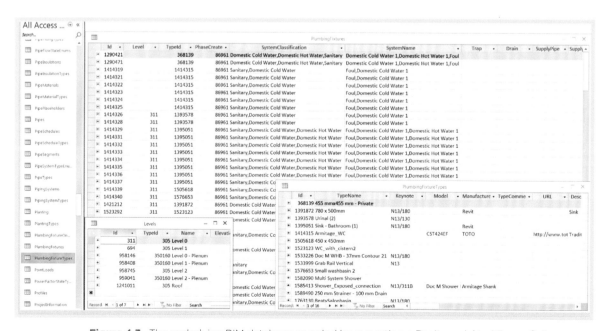

Figure 4.3 The underlying BIM database revealed by exporting a Revit model to Microsoft Access

So, as the building services engineer inserts a plumbing fixture into the model, he or she can also specify its manufacturer, model number, colour, material and catalogue code.

When stored in BIM, this information is database-compatible. (see fig. 4.3) As indicated by the use of the term 'can be managed' above, this data can be integrated and updated using ERP, the enterprise-wide information systems that connect various other business departments, such as planning, manufacturing, sales, marketing, distribution, accounting, human resources, project management, inventory control, and maintenance. This is because, at its heart, BIM is the graphical front end to a database.

Accordingly, if this data represents a level of information that is considered definitive (see Chapter 9), it can be extracted from the model and issued by the contractor to those responsible for procuring construction items and materials.

The challenges of moving to BIM Level 2

The transition to BIM Level 2 is characterised by working in an integrated model environment in order to improve and resolve 3D coordination issues. One of the biggest challenges for the BIM Manager is to encourage the senior project decision-makers responsible for coordination to move from working solely in 2D into the newer and less familiar environment of 3D elements and models.

It should be remembered that this transition to 3D will never signify a complete end to 2D drawing review. Nevertheless, it is a waste of the considerable investment in BIM if some staff members (more often than not the 'old hands') restrict themselves to working in 2D; moreover, this would lead to a situation in which their interaction with the model would remain forever mediated by eager young technicians who are willing to 'chauffeur' them around it. This is certainly not what is intended by BIM level 2; a lack of 3D design review competence among senior designers will severely impair the prospective coordination benefits of BIM.

In order to assess prospective project team members' capability to collaborate in the model, the Employer should insist that a challenging 'real world' coordination practice event is scheduled into the BIM Project Execution Plan (see Chapter 2).

The event should bring together all of those who are responsible for coordination, who should take turns to navigate through a detailed sample federated model, save and mark up views with comments and agreed changes, and then issue instructions for other staff to implement those changes in each discipline's native model. The exercise should conclude by integrating updated model renditions in order that the federated model reflects all of the agreed coordination changes.

The results of the exercise should be followed up by remedial training where necessary. This is important because the British Standards documentation for BIM, PAS-1192, represents this as the most basic level of model interaction for those involved in coordination.

WHAT IS LEVEL 3?

Currently, BIM design software is usually deployed onto individual PCs. As explained above, for BIM Level 2, the Information exchange is by means of file sharing. However, it is clear that, as the level of detail represented in models is refined, file sizes tend to increase beyond practical limits. In order to scale above these limits, information sharing is usually best addressed by implementing a database structure, i.e. schema, instead of sharing discrete files. Unlike individual files, the schema can be distributed and remain coherent across multiple storage devices.

For BIM Level 3, users directly and continuously update a shared building model. Instead of working with proprietary file formats, all model information is organised into a common non-proprietary industry-recognised data structure, known as *Industry Foundation Classes*, or IFC (See 'Open BIM Workflows' in Chapter 8). This method of

Figure 4.4 Collaboration via single shared building model[4]

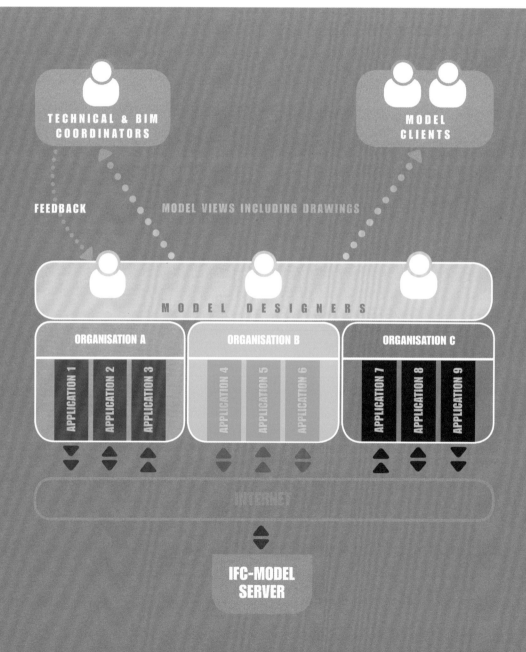

collaboration contrasts sharply with the BIM Level 2 process of periodically *converting* and uploading separate models to the shared project repository for integration into a federated model.

Here the entire model remains accessible, while users can also extract and download partial models from the model server. Segments of the stored model that have been selected and downloaded (checked out) in this way can be amended by a modelling tool and reloaded (checked in) again. At check-in, the partial model is merged into the existing model, such that updated elements replace their existing counterparts on the server, while new objects are added to the existing model and any deleted objects are removed from it.

Beyond just collaborative multi-disciplinary modelling, the database structure of the BIM Level 3 model allows for automated processes.

The purchasing procedure is a familiar construction management process. In the manual scenario, the purchase order is completed by a requestor, then processed by a purchase officer. By contrast, at BIM Level 3, one aspect of the automated process would be for a requestor to be authenticated on the server and to run a web query using criteria that extract quantities and specifications from the on-line IFC construction model. In turn, the server would generate a report triggering a database search for approved suppliers that could match the required specification, availability, lead-time and proximity to site. The link to a Request for Quotation web form would be despatched via an automated email to those suppliers. The uploaded and priced quotations would then be automatically ranked in readiness for placing an actual order with one of them.

Thus, BIM Level 3 provides the data structure for 'self-service' business process automation for building design, construction and operations.

It should be noted that while IFC is critical to BIM Level 3, achieving it consists of far more than simply moving files in that format to a central server.

Digital Built Britain

BIM Level 3 is part of a wider strategy that seeks to combine the benefits of combining the 3D model with operational data acquired through non-proprietary internet-enabled sensors. The latter are being embedded into many manufactured components and systems that will become integral to buildings in the near future.

The Digital Built Britain strategy[5] was announced by the UK Department for Business, Innovation and Skills (BIS) in 2014 and involves a phased introduction of large-scale dataset analysis to interrogate 'real-time' performance-monitoring data that has been superimposed on IFC asset data structures. The strategy will include the following key initiatives:

- In-use performance targets becoming the basis for computer-mediated collaboration in the design, construction and operation of assets
- The comparison of operational performance data with performance predicted by design as the basis for new performance-oriented Design, Build, Operate contractual arrangements
- Extension of model-based design optimisation for manufacture and assembly techniques to infrastructure projects
- Use of data from embedded sensors that monitor performance and condition to yield feedback that is used to optimise asset maintenance regimes
- The eventual provision of city-wide performance analysis to inform urban development strategy
- The development of an international urban performance analysis industry, known as Smart Cities.[6]

The BIM Level 3 Digital Built Britain strategy comprises four stages depicted in fig. 4.5.

BIM Level 3 Impact

While the near-term impact will be an increasing demand for models to be issued in the non-proprietary IFC format, this will not immediately affect existing modes of project delivery. Nevertheless, the introduction of new performance-based contract documents (Level 3B) will be oriented towards comparing the performance predicted in design models with actual operational performance.

In the future, it will be increasingly important for project teams to ensure that the completed asset performance makes good on the final predicted outcomes, such as energy savings, that they have modelled and submitted in BIM.

GOAL SETTING FOR DESIGN AND CONSTRUCTION COLLABORATION IN BIM

Although the government mandate is for BIM Level 2 on all centrally procured government projects by 2016, it should be remembered

Figure 4.5 The four stages of the Digital Built Britain strategy

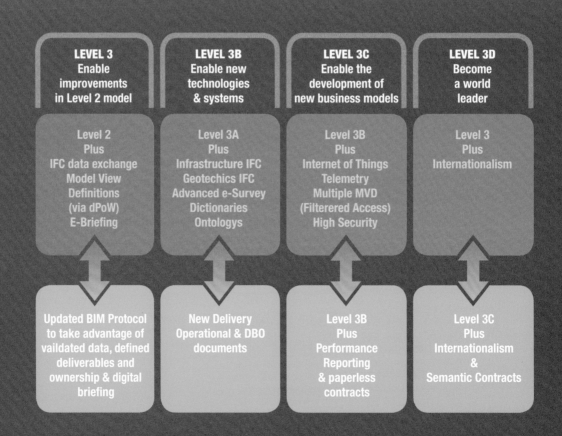

that the purpose of moving to the next maturity level of BIM adoption is to improve the efficiency and effectiveness of the design, construction and handover process.

There remains a danger that firms can become excessively reductive in just seeking to demonstrate Level 2 compliance, while neglecting to see it as a step along a path towards implementing the fullest possible collaborative effort on projects via BIM. That path should not only realistically recognise where each organisation is today, but also indicate a desire to eventually achieve the full collaborative benefits of a BIM Level 2 Strategy.

THE STRATEGIC BENEFITS AND GOALS OF BIM LEVEL 2

As a recap, it's useful to reiterate the key benefits (as highlighted in the Government BIM Strategy) that accrue from successfully adopting BIM technology and processes:

- The implications of alternative design proposals can be evaluated with comparative ease.
- Projects are modelled in three dimensions (eliminating coordination errors and subsequent expensive change).
- Design data can be fed direct to machine tools, creating a link between design and manufacture, and eliminating unnecessary intermediaries.
- There is a proper basis for asset management subsequent to construction.

The high-level goals for any firm that implements BIM should be aligned with this, i.e.

- Improving the ease with which alternative design proposals are evaluated
- Reduction/elimination of coordination errors
- Reduction/elimination of unnecessary intermediate steps between design and construction procurement/manufacture
- Providing a reliable information base for post-construction asset management.

SENIOR SPONSORSHIP AND FIRM-WIDE COMMITMENT

As you consider this list, it's worth imagining what the future might look like for your firm.

1 What would these look like as a set of SMART objectives tailored to each staff level?

2 What sort of preparation and reporting regime would need to be in place for staff to quantify improvements through BIM?

As you wrestle with these questions, you will realise that the achievement of these goals requires senior sponsorship, large-scale resource commitment and a regime of regular progress reporting. In essence, these goals need to become a stated and supported part of the organisation's overall business strategy.

QUANTIFYING SUCCESS

At this point, you should ask yourself how these outcomes are currently measured.

For instance:

1 In respect of comparing proposals, what sort of criteria do you think are the most challenging to communicate and difficult for clients to evaluate? How might BIM improve the quality of visual communication about sustainability strategies, engineering analysis results, proof of fit and coordination for access and maintenance, and cost and programme implications of a design change?

2 Client feedback: Your marketing team should conduct a survey of what representatives of major clients found easy and difficult to evaluate from your most recent proposals for a design change or alternative construction approach.

3 Hold a BIM open day in which you invite client representatives to view a range of additional deliverables derived from the model. Ask for feedback on how the resulting data would affect the ease of evaluating the pros and cons of alternative proposals.

4 Beyond just 3D visualisations, what other kinds of BIM outputs have clients considered in order to facilitate their evaluation of proposals? Graphs? Schedules? Colour-coded plans?

5 Will the cost of implementing these new workflows be recouped on the project, or does the benefit come primarily from improved client relations and the development of a marketable service differentiator?

6 How does your team currently track coordination issues through to resolution? If the course of each discussion is buried in a set of email exchanges, the evidence of reduced error will remain largely anecdotal. For tracking issues to resolution, you should follow customer service best practices by establishing a consistent format for recording the progression of any issues, as well as a protocol for filing and retrieving different types of project-related communications. (In the absence of a dedicated project data management system, emails and project team meeting minutes can still provide a source of data to compare how quickly discussions about coordination are being resolved.)

7 As a shared project resource, how could the federated model and associated design data have significantly reduced the likelihood of coordination issues either arising or being perpetuated?

8 Contact fabricators and investigate the benefit of using the model for off-site manufacture of specific components in order to accelerate aspects of the construction process.

If these steps have been implemented properly and with the leadership of a BIM champion who can galvanise staff-wide commitment, they will provide quantitative evidence of business improvement.

Remember that it remains the firm's prerogative to phase the introduction of these outputs into the design/construction process in a cost-effective manner. It is not acceptable to simply ignore client feedback, or postpone indefinitely any actions that should follow from it.

That said, implementing this goal may require a shift in office culture towards shared project responsibility and performance transparency. If a blame culture holds sway, no-one will want to be open about the amount design re-work and coordination errors that currently occur on projects.

CONCLUSION

We have reviewed the BIM Maturity Levels in terms of how drawings and other project-related data are organised and exchanged between team members. At its most basic, BIM Level 2 is implemented in organisations that develop the project in 3D and use BIM collaboration software as a 'bridge' to combine their exported model renditions into a federated model in readiness for coordination sessions.

The ability to walk through, examine and mark up views within the federated model should not be restricted to enthusiastic technicians. For BIM Level 2, all technical coordinators should be able to use prepared 3D models this way.

BIM Level 2 has a strategic significance for organisations that understand the potential for the kind of data that is embedded in and linked to each model to enhance communication with other business processes. Data from the model can be linked to databases for material procurement, project management schedules, and staff resourcing schedules. It is important for your organisation to identify specific objectives in order to leverage this data for its own benefit and for that of the project.

[1] PAS-1192-2, ©Mervyn Richards and Mark Bew, 2013 (UK), p.vi.

[2] BIM Strategy Paper, BIS BIM Working Party, 2011.

[3] British Standards Institution, BS-1192, Collaborative production of architectural, engineering and construction information – Code of practice, 2007.

[4] Kaj A. Jørgensen. Jørn Skauge, Per Christiansson, Kjeld Svidt, Kristian Birch Sørensen, John Mitchell (Aalborg University), Use of IFC Model Servers: Modelling Collaboration Possibilities in Practice, 2008

[5] Digital Built Britain – Level 3 Building Information Modelling – Strategy, Department for Business, Innovation and Skills, 2014 ©Crown Copyright

[6] Smart Cities Background Paper, Department for Business, Innovation and Skills, 2013 ©Crown Copyright

05

THE CHALLENGES AND BENEFITS OF BIM COORDINATION: 3D, 4D AND 5D

INTRODUCTION

The goal of coordination is to achieve comprehensive and pre-emptive coherence of design and construction. This is as important within each specialty as it is across all disciplines, drawing types and scales. Incoherent design is not only costly and time-consuming to rectify on site. It is also unsafe.

There are two means by which BIM can facilitate this effort:
* Computer automation
* Computer assistance.

This chapter explores these methods as well as the key challenges involved and actual processes employed in using BIM to achieve design coherence spatially (3D), sequentially (4D) and quantitatively (5D).

The key coverage of this chapter is as follows;
* Coordination challenges
* The practical steps involved in coordination through BIM.

COORDINATION CHALLENGES

Coordination involves a regime of preventive scrutiny. It seeks to eliminate incoherent communication in design and construction. Comprehensive coordination may be sub-divided into five distinct challenges:
* Drawing set coordination and scale-appropriate drawing contents
* Coordination with survey position of the existing and proposed building, its zones and phases
* Safety, accessibility, operations and maintenance (O & M) provisions
* Adequacy of the spatial provision, construction sequence and quantities required for the intended design and construction of elements belonging to each discipline
* Adequacy of the complementary provision, including clearances, for the intended construction interfaces between disciplines.

There are six key aspects to the elimination of coordination errors:
* For each deliverable type, prior agreement on consistent documented standards, templates and approved exemplars
* For all disciplines, prior agreement on sheet sizes and scales, projected sheet lists and consistently named and located zones that will ensure adequate drawing coverage for the project at the required scale
* Pre-defined project-specific element libraries to accommodate the full range of deliverables and drawing scales
* Appropriate balance between detail automatically derived from 3D elements and that which is routinely applied through 2D drafting and annotations
* Adequate internal cycles of scrutiny to ensure coherence across all aspects of design intent
* Cycles of project team scrutiny to ensure that all disciplines have made adequate

complementary provisions for each other as well as clearances for safety, accessibility, operations and maintenance.

WHY USE BIM?

There are 10 key ways in which BIM facilitates coherent output in a way that is much more difficult to implement through multiple separate CAD files. They can be divided into two categories: those automated by the computer and those assisted by the computer. The latter require additional visual scrutiny.

Computer automated coordination

1 **Model updates concurrently:** Multiple users work concurrently, changing the geometry, position and parameters of elements. When synchronised, these changes automatically update the elements and associated annotations for every other user. This is much faster than sequentially updating and coordinating individual drawings.

2 **Element and view re-use:** By linking models, every aspect of the appearance of views and elements in models of one

Figure 5.1 Concurrent updates to the Central Model in BIM

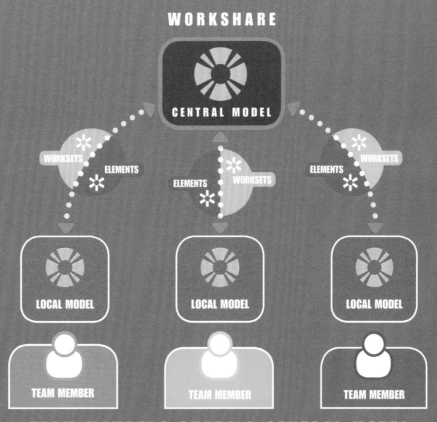

discipline can be re-used as an automatic background by other disciplines. This is an immediate time-saver.

3 **Consistency across drawing scales:** Orthographic large-scale views (1:500 and 1:200) of 3D elements are consistent with those in the smaller-scale views (e.g. 1:50 and 1:20 detail views) derived from them.

4 **Project-wide datums:** Reference datums (like grids and levels) and model elements are presented consistently in multiple view types (e.g. plans, RCPs, section, elevation,

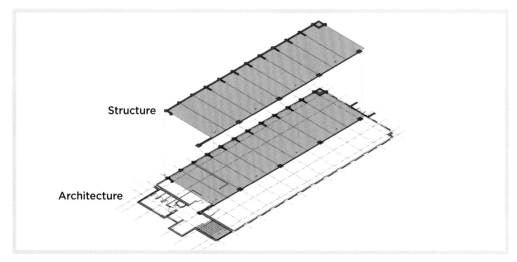

Figure 5.2 Views and elements from structural model re-used in architectural GAs[2]

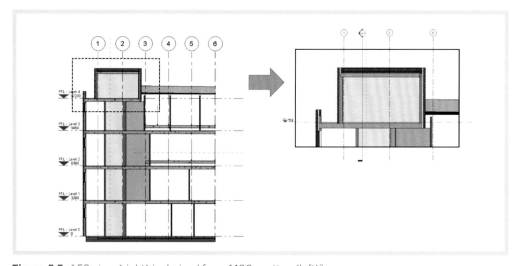

Figure 5.3 1:50 view (right) is derived from 1:100 section (left)[2]

details) and linked models. Therefore, they can be re-used without re-drawing, thereby ensuring consistent positioning throughout the entire project.

5 **Drawing zone consistency:** Several BIM software features will save views representing consistent overlapping areas on each level for general arrangement drawing production. For example, Autodesk Revit has the rectangular scope box that controls the view boundary on multiple levels. For those using Bentley Aecosim, there are saved views boundaries, while Graphisoft ArchiCAD provides Model View Options. These features enable the preparation of drawings that can be read coherently.

6 **View templates:** In one model file, view and sheet templates can be applied to multiple views in order to maintain consistent presentation standards across the entire drawing set.

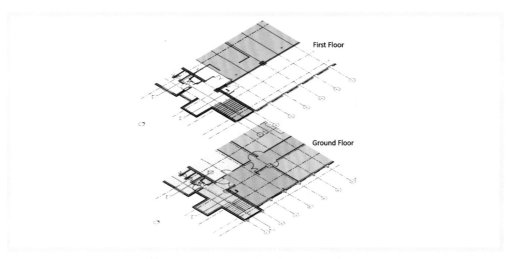

Figure 5.4 Project-wide grid lines are consistent for all floor levels[2]

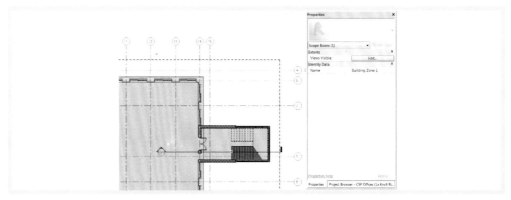

Figure 5.5 Revit scope box used to control grid line offsets[2]

7 **Drawing cross-reference automation:** When sections, elevations and other details are placed on sheets, the corresponding drawing symbols are automatically cross-referenced with the correct numbers for view and sheet.

Computer-assisted coordination

8 **Resolving complex interferences and construction sequences:** As they increase in detail and complexity, multi-disciplinary interface provisions, clearances and

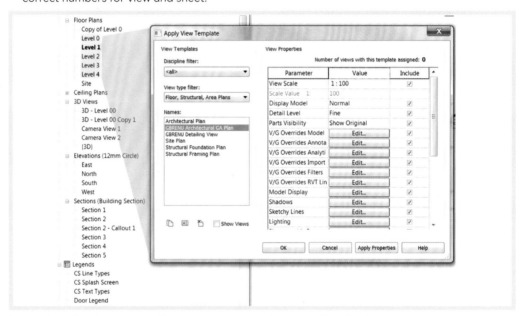

Figure 5.6 View template applies consistent properties to multiple drawing views[2]

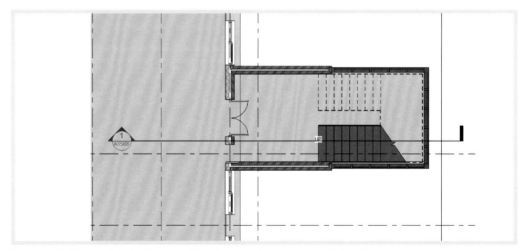

Figure 5.7 Section label automatically references the associated sheet[2]

construction sequences become easier to understand and resolve in an integrated 3D environment than on multiple separate 2D plans, sections and elevations. While the computer can identify clashes and clearances between elements, some of these may arise from differences in the level of detail. The roof might still be modelled monolithically, and therefore overlap elements from the structural model. For computer-assisted co-ordination, visual scrutiny will work, establishing that structural cross-bracing is in the wrong position because it is positioned in front of a window.

9 **Schedules**: Items of furniture, fittings and equipment (FF&E) can be scheduled by room. MEP schedules will automatically reveal items which do not belong to a defined building system. The continuity of design performance requirements (e.g. fire and acoustic rating) can be automatically distinguished by colour coding. Technical coordinators can quickly locate all unconnected equipment and ensure that it is adequately supported and connected to the correct services.

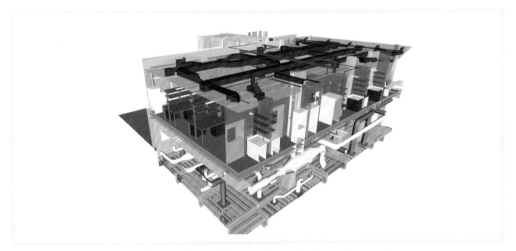

Figure 5.8 Structural model (green) must be coordinated with architecture[2]

Room	Number	Description	W1	W2	H1	H2	H3	H4
Office Space	2	Generic-Metric (Int. Uneven (926 x XXX) - Flush Panel)	926	526	2040	1528	2085	2085
Ladies Toilet	3	Generic-Metric (Int. Single - Flush Panel)	726		2040	800	2085	2085
Ladies Toilet	4	Generic-Metric (Int. Single - Flush Panel)	626		2040	700	2085	2085
Ladies Toilet	5	Generic-Metric (Int. Single - Flush Panel)	626		2040	700	2085	2085
Ladies Toilet	6	Generic-Metric (Int. Single - Flush Panel)	626		2040	700	2085	2085
Ladies Toilet	7	Generic-Metric (Int. Single - Flush Panel)	726		2040	800	2085	2085
Ladies Toilet	8	Generic-Metric (Int. Double - Flush Panel)	426	426	2040	928	2085	2085
Ladies Toilet	9	Generic-Metric (Int. Double - Flush Panel)	426	426	2040	928	2085	2085
Room	10	Generic-Metric 100mm Frame (Int. Double - Flush Panel)	526	526	2040	1128	2085	2085
Open Plan 2	11	Generic-Metric (Int. Single - Flush Panel)	826		2040	900	2085	2085
Open Plan 2	12	Generic-Metric (Int. Uneven (926 x XXX) - Flush Panel)	926	526	2040	1528	2085	2085
Ladies Toilet	13	Generic-Metric (Int. Single - Flush Panel)	726		2040	800	2085	2085
Ladies Toilet	14	Generic-Metric (Int. Single - Flush Panel)	626		2040	700	2085	2085
Ladies Toilet	15	Generic-Metric (Int. Single - Flush Panel)	626		2040	700	2085	2085
Ladies Toilet	16	Generic-Metric (Int. Single - Flush Panel)	626		2040	700	2085	2085
Ladies Toilet	17	Generic-Metric (Int. Single - Flush Panel)	726		2040	800	2085	2085
Ladies Toilet	18	Generic-Metric (Int. Double - Flush Panel)	426	426	2040	928	2085	2085
Ladies Toilet	19	Generic-Metric (Int. Double - Flush Panel)	426	426	2040	928	2085	2085
Room	20	Generic-Metric 100mm Frame (Int. Double - Flush Panel)	526	526	2040	1128	2085	2085
Annexe	40	Generic-Metric (Int. Single - Flush Panel)	826		2040	900	2085	2085
Toilet	23	Generic-Metric (Int. Single - Flush Panel)	726		2040	800	2085	2085
Toilet	24	Generic-Metric (Int. Single - Flush Panel)	626		2040	700	2085	2085
Toilet	25	Generic-Metric (Int. Single - Flush Panel)	626		2040	700	2085	2085
Toilet	26	Generic-Metric (Int. Single - Flush Panel)	626		2040	700	2085	2085
Toilet	27	Generic-Metric (Int. Single - Flush Panel)	726		2040	800	2085	2085
Toilet	28	Generic-Metric (Int. Double - Flush Panel)	426	426	2040	928	2085	2085
Toilet	29	Generic-Metric (Int. Double - Flush Panel)	426	426	2040	928	2085	2085

Figure 5.9 Door schedule that automatically updates with changes to the model[2]

Again, despite these benefits, there remains a need to scrutinise the schedules to identify extraneous and uncoordinated items.

10 **Material quantity schedules:** These will facilitate early quantities for off-site construction and preliminary estimates. Again, the computer will extract quantities from monolithic elements, but will not automatically divide up these quantities into the categories of an industry-standard work breakdown structure, such as the New Rules of Measurement 2.

WHAT CAN GO WRONG?

Implementing BIM poorly can lead to difficulties in coordination. Some examples of common mistakes are listed below.

1 **Lack of execution on BIM project execution plans:** BIM project execution plans define the output standards, the deliverables that will be required from the model and the approach that will be used to produce them to those standards. Failure to implement the plan will lead to incoherent drawing sets caused by inconsistencies in the content of similar drawing types, misunderstandings about how many of each type of drawing is required and the amount of detail to be specified in each. The result is an inconsistently presented and poorly annotated design.

2 **Lack of user control when inserting elements:** Inexperienced users may insert elements in their correct plan location, but without adequately checking on their 3D coordination in elevation. This is especially true for FF&E, stepped paving and stairs. While this control is not needed when producing a 2D plan drawing by itself, it is essential for working in the 3D environment. Ensuring continuous spatial coordination may require the use of an additional graphics monitor that enables the model to be clearly depicted across two screens showing its orthographic and 3D views simultaneously.

3 **Collaborating firms underuse the linking of each other's models:** Firms that lack a process for regularly integrating each other's model changes will end up working with outdated information and laboriously re-creating (instead of re-using) each

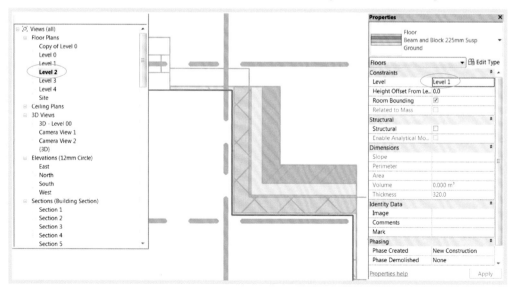

Figure 5.10 Plan of floor slab mistakenly inserted on level 1 in level 2 view[2]

other's model elements and views. The point of collaboration is for firms to build on each other's efforts; the re-creation of elements that have already been modelled elsewhere wastes time and resources.

4 **Underuse of project-wide reference coordinates:** Each discipline works to its own reference levels, grids and geometry, instead of sharing the same datums and coordinates. In many cases, as the result of several changes to each discipline's levels, these coordinates no longer match up.

5 **Neglect of 3D model review:** Preference for 2D drawing reviews alone (as was customary before BIM) and aversion to the 3D environment can hinder the BIM benefits of making detailed and complex interfaces between elements more easily understood. Often, this preference is expressed by reviewers constantly asking for other staff to print out drawings on their behalf. It is wasteful for those involved in design to be tasked with printing drawings on behalf of other staff who could learn to do it for themselves. This is no more acceptable than a member of staff expecting a colleague to print out emails on his or her behalf. Everyone in the design process should be trained and capable of viewing and printing a drawing sheet that has been set up in the organisation's default BIM design application.

6 **Neglect of schedules:** BIM schedules provide a helpful checklist of items, especially those needing complementary structural and MEP systems, interface provisions and clearances. Without using schedules extensively, technical coordinators rely upon visual scrutiny alone, which is more time-consuming and risk-prone.

7 **Insufficient model element detail:** Simplified elements, such as those comprising a wall-floor junction modelled at early design stages, must be increased in detail for construction purposes. If these 3D elements remain under-developed, every single small-scale drawing will need to be updated with time-consuming overlays of 2D drafting.

8 **Over-detailed 3D elements:** Rather than creating 3D elements (especially furniture) from scratch, it is often easier to download these elements from the web and insert them as placeholders into a model. The level of detail in these is often more appropriate to later design stages; using them too early in the project can lead to a bloated model. The latter results in slow access and printing, and unresponsive model navigation. Downloaded 3D content should be vetted before use in the model, especially in terms of file size. Unnecessary detail should be stripped out. (In major BIM packages, there are software controls for these elements that can vary what is visible at coarse, medium and fine levels of detail.)

9 **Users neglect visibility 'power tools', such as view templates:** Drafting standards can be embedded in view templates that can, in turn, be applied to multiple views of the same scale and type. The neglect of these tools results in inefficient control of the many views that are used to produce multiple project drawings and schedules. As a result, users spend too much time amending each view in order to maintain visual consistency between several sheets in a drawing set.

THE PRACTICAL STEPS INVOLVED IN COORDINATION THROUGH BIM

So, assuming that the above issues have been resolved, let us consider the practical processes involved in eliminating coordination errors through BIM.

COORDINATION ROLES

The PAS-1192-2 documentation provides guidance and illustrations to explain how spatial coordination should be conducted in BIM. Key to this is the role of the task team, which PAS-1192-2 describes in this way:

'Task Teams are any team assembled to complete a TASK.'

'Examples: Architectural Task Team; Structural Task Team or multi-disciplinary Task Team to design a specialist part of the project, say a bespoke curtain wall. This may also include the specialist and professional design teams collaborating to complete that task.'

It goes on to state that meetings for spatial coordination utilising BIM will bring together three distinct roles (Chapter 6, Table 6.1):

- **Technical coordinators (for each discipline and specialty):** In PAS-1192, these are termed task team interface managers.
- **Lead Designer's Project Architect/ Engineer:** These may be called upon to arbitrate otherwise unresolved design issues.
- **BIM Coordinators:** Responsible for preparing the models for spatial coordination meetings.

While project architects, engineers and technical co-ordinators are familiar participants in coordination meetings, the use of the model will be facilitated by the BIM Coordinator. Typically, the BIM Coordinator would be a senior technician on the project, well versed in the key coordination issues and capable of setting up and navigating through the model.

PREPARATION FOR THE MODEL COORDINATION PROCESS

There are a number of key steps involved in preparing for the organised exchange of models for coordination:

1. Sub-divide the overall project into several models distinguished by volume and discipline, or specialty. Tabulate development responsibility for each model over the course of the project (see Chapter 2, Table 2.4). The decision about what type of file to share is based on the permitted purpose agreed in the BIM protocol. For spatial coordination, all that is required is to provide each model in a format that can be opened by the application defined in the Post-Contract BIM Execution Plan for accomplishing that purpose (see Chapter 2, Table 2.1).

2. Establish a Common Data Environment, i.e. a secure, managed and mutually accessible project repository capable of storing and sharing all models and issuing update notifications about them to project participants.

3. Establish a file naming protocol to easily distinguish each model contribution, including its revision status. (see 'Using a data storage naming protocol' in Chapter 3). Define status codes that communicate its suitability for a given purpose, such as review or coordination see Chapter 8, section entitled *Assigning and notifying of model status.*

4. At agreed regular intervals, and on request, each discipline's project lead (known as the task team leader) should approve one or more work-in-progress models for sharing with others, but only after reviewing and approving the derived output.

5. These models are then uploaded to the Common Data Environment in compliance with the agreed timing, standards and naming convention specified in the Post-Contract BIM Project Execution Plan. An update notification should be automatically issued to other project participants.

CLASH AVOIDANCE, DETECTION AND RESOLUTION

Preventing clashes is a far better strategy than fixing those that could have been avoided in the first place. The project team's approach to coordination should prioritise clash avoidance.

1. Typically, clashes can be avoided by pre-assigning the locations and routes of each discipline's work to particular building zones and levels. Major runs of primary ductwork should be assigned to specific riser locations, while secondary distribution should be assigned to specific levels in the ceiling. On this basis, clashes should only occur at points of exit from and access to service risers. For BIM Level 2, a proprietary application – such as Bentley Navigator®, Autodesk Navisworks®, Tekla BIMsight® and Solibri Model Checker® – should be used to provide a unified view of the combined multi-disciplinary (i.e. federated) model. A key feature of such applications is the ability to identify interferences between components – i.e. clash detection. In testing for these, selection criteria are applied to reveal specific types of clashes, such as occur between structure, partitions and pipework, or between ceilings and ductwork.

2 Spatial coordination meetings should be scheduled and chaired by the technical coordinator for the Lead Designer. In PAS-1192-2, technical coordinators are described as 'task team interface managers'. On behalf of their respective teams, their role is to meet regularly and ensure that all disciplines have made adequate complementary provisions for each other and clearances for safety, accessibility, operations and maintenance.

For spatial coordination, technical coordinators should visually inspect both combined multi-disciplinary models and the drawings that have been derived from them. Assistance in touring the 3D environment should be provided by role of BIM coordinator. As outlined earlier, this is not necessarily a dedicated BIM Manager, but instead a technician on the project who has demonstrated a high aptitude, after initial training, for producing design deliverables and for touring and setting up views in the 3D model.

When conflicts or the lack of complementary provisions are detected, the technical coordinators' role is to decide and record the design changes that will be required to resolve these clashes. If they reach an impasse, the lead designer's project architect or engineer is responsible for arbitrating these design decisions.

3 Once the design changes that are needed to resolve a clash have been agreed and approved, the technical coordinators should implement them through their respective design teams. The work-in-progress models will be updated and the resulting revisions shared with notifications of changes through the Common Data Environment.

4 After downloading the revised models and in conjunction with the BIM coordinator, each technical coordinator should conduct a final check to ensure that the agreed design changes are reflected in each model.

CONSTRUCTION COORDINATION IN BIM: 4D

The coordination of construction processes can be improved by using BIM software to link elements in the model to tasks created in a project management application. This creates a time-lapse animation of the building sequence in which elements will become visible in the same relative order as their respective tasks are organised in the construction sequence. The time dimension is added to the 3D model and explains why this is called 4D.

Benefits of 4D

In one sense, contractors 'design' the construction sequences needed to build the completed facility. A key benefit of 4D simulation is that its resemblance to the physical reality makes it easy for all stakeholders and the whole project team to evaluate alternative construction processes in terms of relative speed, effectiveness and safety.

Typically, on large and centrally procured projects this will involve integrating the detailed logistics from the project schedule of a complex multi-tier supply chain with the 3D model. Nevertheless, the use of 4D is equally valuable to SMEs for reviewing different options for smaller refurbishment projects, by visualising alternatives for the phasing of the decant and handing back of completed parts of the building.

'Forward-thinking design and construction teams also use 4D to match an indicative assembly sequence to their models and thereby explain the order of element assembly needed to complete the project.

For instance, on the King Abdullah University of Science and Technology (KAUST) project, the Revit® design model was re-developed by Oger International and Gehry Technologies in CATIA® as a detailed virtual constructional model.

4D animations were then developed that showed project managers and site operatives exactly how the complex construction

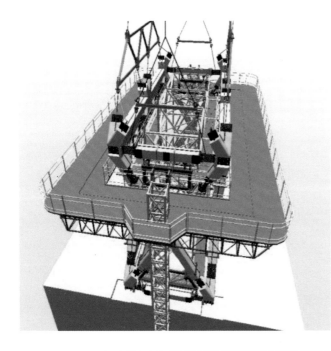

sequence for the solar tower could be implemented effectively and safely.' (see figs 5.11 and 5.12)

WHAT DATA IS REQUIRED FOR 4D?

The development of a 4D simulation requires the integration of two key software resources:

1 3D model of the project, divided into constructional detail.

2 Project management application file containing a schedule of tasks, abridged to correlate to the level of detail in the associated model.

Early on in the project lifecycle, the model will only contain elements that convey the architectural and engineering intentions of the design suppliers. This *design intent model* might be useful for creating an indicative animation sequence, but it will not contain elements representative of each task in the construction programme.

In contrast, the *virtual construction model* replaces the design intent model being developed in further detail by the main contractor working in conjunction with its supply chain. Elements, previously modelled monolithically, must be sub-divided by storey height and movement joints, and into assembly and pre-cast components. Element sub-division would be implemented either through a function of the native application, or in the BIM coordination application itself.

There will also be a requirement to model additional site elements, including:

• Existing buildings and other site topography (if not modelled already)

• Temporary buildings and erected site machinery

• Scaffolding and falsework.

As PAS-1192-2 explains, *'the Project Information Model is developed firstly as a design intent model, showing the architectural and engineering intentions of the design.'*

Figure 5.11 and 5.12 a view of the model showing the construction sequence on KAUST and an actual photo of the construction site[3]

suppliers. Then the PIM is developed into a virtual construction model containing all the objects to be manufactured, installed or constructed.'

Challenges of matching model elements to project management software task data

Creating the 4D animation involves matching imported project scheduling tasks to model elements. In terms of available data, it might seem easy enough for the BIM Manager to obtain the latest project schedule in a compatible format from the Project Manager, and import this into the 4D software along with a rendition of the 3D model appropriate to the required simulation detail. Nevertheless, these inputs are not necessarily useable without significant amendment.

For instance, the complete schedule would typically cover the entire project duration and contain far more detail about indirect site activities and milestones than those relating directly to the construction process and to the current level of model detail.

Also, it is a challenge to produce a 4D animation for simulating a sequence of coatings or surface treatments. Typically, these are part of the specification, but they are not modelled in 3D. In the use of Autodesk Navisworks, this is addressed by extending the range of appearance definitions such that, during the animation, each treatment is represented by a distinct colour change.

Tips for implementing 4D successfully within your firm

Below are a number of initiatives that would facilitate the adoption of 4D.

1   Develop a preparatory 4D awareness campaign using data from a smaller existing project. This would take time to produce, but once complete, it would allow end-users to see the benefits of 4D in simulated project meeting workshops. At the end of each workshop, attendees can be surveyed to gain feedback on the value of the technology.
In this exercise, it would be useful to identify some familiar project scenarios and develop alternative construction sequences for them in 4D. Accomplishing this involves the BIM sponsor and BIM champion (Chapter 3, section entitled *Leadership roles in firms that are new to BIM*) joining forces to gain the commitment of time and effort from other staff to provide realistic scenarios and help in developing useful 4D alternatives to address them.
The authors of a study entitled *BIM and 4D Planning: a holistic study of the barriers and drivers to widespread adoption*[1] highlighted the fact that the adoption of 4D in construction planning was directly attributable to bridging the gap between the technology, end-users and their existing processes. In contrast, many BIM managers spend too much time teaching staff how to create and update the model and not enough time familiarising the design team on how the model would be used in a realistic project context.

2   Refine the use of 4D on projects modelled in BIM into a number of specific advantageous and quantifiable objectives:

a   In the BIM Project Execution Plan, mandate the use of a global Task ID parameter on all elements in all models. Use component schedules to check on this regularly.

b   After reviewing the project schedule, use named selection sets to group elements by the related task and assign to them the correct Task ID value.

c   At the beginning of the construction phase, add elements to a model representing site features, facilities and topography prior to excavation. Combine this with the 3D design intent model to produce the virtual construction model. Develop a 4D simulation of the high-level baseline project plan to complement presentations explaining the overall construction sequence.

d   Categorise sub-element visibility for each model element into coarse, medium and fine display (see Chapter 9 on Level of Definition). This allows the model to revert and be export to a lower level of detail that matches the task detail required for producing 4D.

e   For the first few months of project meetings in the construction phase, collaborate with the construction manager on monthly post-meeting 4D visualisations showing major changes to this baseline schedule as a visual comparison with actual construction progress.

f   In later months and prior to team meetings, confer with the construction manager to produce 4D simulations of major alternatives for the project schedule, especially those showing how time could be recouped.

g   Work with the mechanical contractor's detailed programme to produce a sample 4D animation of a plant room construction sequence.

h   Establish a programme of progressively more detailed modelling efforts over the next two years, dividing ever more of the model's major monolithic elements into construction parts for use in 4D. These would include slab bays, sections of jump-formed structures and unitised partition system lengths.

QUANTIFICATION IN BIM: 5D

Quantification in BIM can range from automated comparison of the schedule of accommodation against design areas (i.e. programme validation) to room-by-room FF&E schedules to the extraction of material quantities.

It is important to distinguish elemental cost planning (which, during design development, divides the project cost into the distinct functions provided by the scheme) from estimating (which contractors use to quantify the materials, labour and equipment needed to complete a construction project).

Cost schedules are automatically derived from BIM by linking unit costs to corresponding components of the model. This capability

yields better result in counting items, than applying the standard methods of measurement to them. Yet, both require a regime of regularly purging the model of extraneous elements. Otherwise, the schedule will count additional items that have been inadvertently inserted into the model and that are superfluous to the design intent.

Scheduling quantities from BIM also does not obviate reliance upon professional surveying expertise to carry out building cost planning. This work includes measurement of the facilitating and contractor designed works, inclusion of the provisional sums, preliminaries, contingencies and non-measurable items that must also be considered.

CHALLENGES OF 5D BIM

There are six main challenges involved in deriving 'real world' benefits from 5D BIM:

*   The grouping and breakdown of model components into their respective cost analysis elements depends on the level of definition (see Chapter 9). The process of extracting quantities can be hampered by a lack of sufficient detail. Also, the design team is not focused on developing the model in a way that ensures that its constituents will always be assigned to the correct cost categories.

*   In the Standard Form of Cost Analysis, there are inclusions and exclusions for each element definition. For instance, as a part of substructure, the lowest floor construction (section 1.1.3) does not include basement walls. The latter should be categorised with external walls (section 2.5). Equally, raised access flooring is grouped with Floor finishes (section 3.2), instead of Floors (section 2.2.1).

*   Dimensional parameters of model elements do not automatically yield the required measurement data. For example, for cost analysis, the elemental quantity for slabs is gross internal floor area (to the inner face of the external wall); by contrast, the larger area derived from the model is measured to the slab perimeter. Again, downstand and

upstand floor beams are not grouped with the Frame (section 2.1), but with the Upper Floors (section 2.2).

- There is a need to provide specification and design criteria to indicate the required performance of each element. This data will inform the unit cost calculation.
- It may be difficult to divide the finishes of continuous walls and floors extending beyond individual rooms. Some finishes might not even be modelled, but instead be added into the specification.
- Construction classification systems need to be rationalised to allow models to interoperate between them. Uniclass 2 is currently the definitive system for the construction specification in the UK, whereas the New Rules of Measurement 2, used for cost classification, is structured differently.

In order to address these challenges, the BIM Manager must make a strategic reckoning to identify where exactly the effort required to break down and re-group 3D model elements represents a significant improvement on traditional methods of measurement that use 2D drawings. This would be where BIM processes impart either greater speed or accuracy than would be achievable by the latter.

In many cases, it is preferable to employ a hybrid approach that integrates the benefits of 5D BIM with traditional costing techniques. 5D is best used for approximations that help decision-makers compare the cost impact of various design and construction alternatives and to quantify FF&E accurately.

CONCLUSION

In terms of reducing the significant costs incurred by rework and to improve the understanding and safety of proposed methods, coordination should be at the heart of BIM Level 2 implementation.

The BIM Project Execution Plan should clearly define the benefits, scope, normative processes and outputs of 3D, 4D and 5D BIM.

Within each firm, the BIM Sponsor and BIM Champion must develop and implement a gradual programme of BIM awareness sessions to familiarise staff with these model outputs by simulating the experience (beyond static visualisations and drawings) of using them. They should also spearhead the gradual incorporation of the technology into project coordination meetings and planning processes.

The next chapter considers how this transition is effected through organisational change.

---

[1] Kassem, Brogden and Dawood, *BIM and 4D Planning: a holistic study of the barriers and drivers to widespread adoption*, 2012
[2] Autodesk screen shots reprinted with the permission of Autodesk, Inc.
[3] Images courtesy of Gehry Technologies and HOK

MANAGING THE MANDATE: THE BIM LEVEL 2 ENVIRONMENT

INTRODUCTION

Although the Levels of BIM Maturity were outlined in Chapter 4, it is important to address the impact on the organisation as it seeks to adopt BIM Level 2. In this chapter, BIM Level 2 is explained in terms of managing the organisational change and implementation plan required to deliver it.

This includes:

* What does BIM Level 2 mean for my organisation?
* BIM Manager's essential project delivery task list.

WHAT DOES BIM LEVEL 2 MEAN FOR MY ORGANISATION?

The title of this section is probably the question that the construction industry asks more than any other, in terms of the mandate for fully collaborative 3D BIM on all centrally procured UK government construction projects. In order to understand the impact on the organisation, it is important to consider the key internal environment factors that will be affected. These are:

* Organisational culture
* Management
* Organisational structure
* Assets
* Financial strength
* Human resources.

ORGANISATIONAL CULTURE

Culture has been described as a *'system of shared assumptions, values, and beliefs that show employees what is appropriate and inappropriate behaviour.'* [1]

In respect of adopting new initiatives like BIM, the organisational culture must beget an atmosphere of trust, which means relying on the honesty and integrity of others, especially the leadership. Unlike business as usual, multi-faceted technologies like BIM will pervade every aspect of design and construction practice; their successful implementation will therefore require the cohesive effort of the entire company.

If trust in the leadership is lacking, there will be misgivings about any managerial assertions about the smoothness of changing over to BIM and whether transitional arrangements will be sufficient for the level of responsibility accepted by those adopting the new technology.

Organisational culture influences whether staff respond to management initiatives with enthusiasm, indifference or complete apathy – is typically informed by past experiences. Whether good or bad, these can make or break future attempts to deploy new technology.

As an example, let us describe a situation in a hypothetical organisation, where some previous IT implementations, including a sophisticated project data management solution, have foundered badly due to insufficient investment in configuration, professional support and training. Despite this, end-users might still have unofficially borne the brunt of blame for the failure of the new systems. On that basis, the same end-users would be justifiably wary of unqualified managerial optimism about realising the benefits of BIM.

As a means of engendering trust, management should announce their plans for BIM only after they have factored professional support, training and realistic staff development timescales into the overall impact of implementation. They should establish a monthly office-wide forum for raising concerns and agreeing solutions in relation to the new technology. A BIM 'suggestion box' would also provide a means for staff to air issues anonymously. This kind of interaction would help to develop genuine and collective consensus and trust.

MANAGEMENT: DEVELOPING A CONSENSUS TO INFORM YOUR STRATEGIC AIMS FOR BIM LEVEL 2 IMPLEMENTATION

Consider the below example of exporting the data in the 3D model of a major hospital to a Microsoft Access database. The resulting equipment database was sorted by level, filtered and enumerated.

This demonstrates that, beyond 3D, models can be used to embed and exchange commercially valuable information about every aspect of the design, construction and operation of built assets in a format that is spatially organised and also searchable by normal database queries.

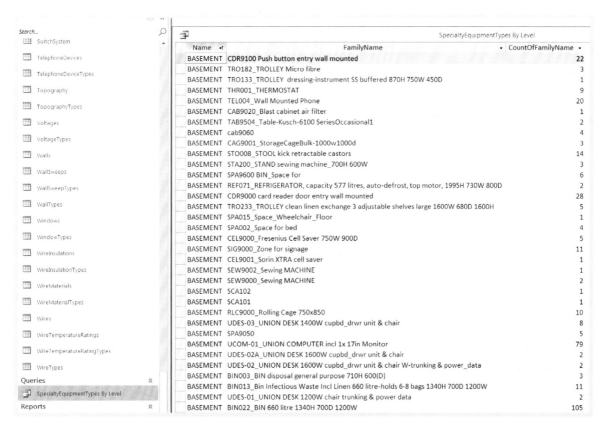

Figure 6.1 Database export of the 3D model

This is of immense value in helping to achieve major improvements in both inter-departmental and inter-organisational efficiency. Therefore, BIM warrants the full involvement of senior management in committing firm-wide time, effort and other resources to its successful implementation.

The first step is for senior management to arrive at a consensus on the reasons that BIM Level 2 is an important corporate goal, how it fits into the overall corporate strategy, and the timescale and criteria for monitoring how it is achieved. What are the risks involved (including that of doing nothing)?

This consensus should be the basis for defining the firm's strategic aims for BIM. For example, they might include:

1   To remain competitive by alignment with the evolving external business environment in which BIM will be a mandatory requirement by 2016.

2   Reduction of costs (including rework) by exchanging project information in a computer-based environment that facilitates coordination by cross-referencing, analysing and visualising shared and spatially organised design, construction and asset data.

3   The development of new opportunities by marketing the capabilities to use BIM to provide fully coordinated design, construction and asset data.

    The organisation's vision statement is an important outcome from this consensus on BIM strategy. The vision should encapsulate the ideal positioning in the competitive business environment that should result from your strategic efforts.

Here are a few examples of BIM vision statements, some of which align closely with the above-mentioned aims:

- Fully coordinated multi-disciplinary design in BIM by 2016
- Recognised leadership in cost-effective construction through BIM
- Superior knowledge management of client design standards through BIM.

Reminding staff of the Vision

The vision must be articulated regularly and consistently by senior staff as a set of clear long-term strategic goals combined with the consequent measurable objectives and key performance indicators that need to be achieved (see Chapter 1).

Creating a Readiness Assessment

Once the goals have been clarified, the management team should commission the BIM Sponsor, in conjunction with an external consultancy with a proven BIM implementation track record, to develop a documented assessment of the current state of the firm and its readiness to implement BIM. This would include:

- As a pre-cursor to Level 2, the extent to which the firm has already achieved BIM Level 1 maturity (i.e. managed CAD within a common data environment of consistently organised project-wide data and drawings).

- The significance of achieving BIM Level 2 to the firm's current and future prospects (the resultant report would review client demand, competitiveness and government compliance, and draw upon case study comparisons with similar organisations that demonstrate the range of improvements in market opportunities, efficiency of collaboration and coordination that can be achieved through BIM).

- The potential for the firm to capitalise on new marketing opportunities arising from BIM.

- Evaluation of the impact of the BIM initiative in changing, sustaining, or furthering market position, existing staff roles and organisational capabilities.

- The key performance indicators that will be used to evaluate success, alongside an evaluation of current project information management processes' effectiveness.

- A flowchart of demonstrable proposed BIM workflows that will improve efficiency both internal and externally.

- For the achievement of BIM Level 2 objectives, an approximate schedule with key investment points for phasing the introduction of BIM in a manner that would provide sufficient time for the entire organisation to adapt to the new technology.

- Evaluation of organisational optimism or concerns about the BIM initiative and the proposed response to them.

- Any new roles that might be required to support the organisational implementation of BIM Level 2, for example, the roles of BIM Coordinator and Information Manager.

- A matrix detailing the relative capabilities (3D, 4D, 5D: see Chapter 5), costs and compatibility of industry-recognised BIM applications, including licensing, hardware/ network requirements, deployment approaches, training and support offered at all levels of usage.

- A realistic proposed budget to cover the first three years of deployment, including software licenses, training and support, new staff, documenting new processes and standards, and upgrades to existing hardware and IT infrastructure.

- The person who is considered best suited to the prospective role of BIM Champion.

Creating an Implementation Plan and Organisational Structure

A BIM implementation plan should be developed by the BIM Sponsor and BIM Champion (see Chapter 3) after reviewing the readiness assessment. In particular, the plan should contain the following elements:

- Roles and responsibilities and organisational structure in support of BIM workflow

- Overview of the proposed system, including the phasing of licenses and hardware upgrades

- Glossary explaining BIM jargon in plain English

- Implementation tasks:
  - Formation of the in-house and externally contracted BIM implementation project team. Contact details and description of roles, responsibilities and authorities.
  - Scheduled visits and meetings held before, during and after implementation.
  - Cost breakdown and defined programme for planning and coordinating the implementation.
  - Prerequisite milestones to be achieved before the implementation date.
  - Outlines of learning paths and training appropriate to various BIM uses and levels in the project team (from awareness sessions to new users to power-user/administrators).
  - Development of a pilot project model and templates to produce deliverables that are representative of existing production standards.
  - Model setup and support in using BIM coordination tools for team meetings.
  - Checklists of IT information required to implement the software (server names, network configuration, deployment configurations, etc.).
  - Documentation of the implemented system, training manuals, standards and collaboration process maps that are applicable to the implementation effort.
  - Establishment of internal technical/ IT support and backup procedures, software provider's support and service level agreements.
  - Required upgrades to other software, hardware or network configuration.
  - Scheduling of any specialised computer configuration required prior to implementation.
  - Potential legacy data conversion in order to maintain compatibility with the new system.
  - Organisational authority for reviewing and approving the Plan.

The implementation plan – with a realistic budget and schedule – should be reviewed by the directors and either rejected, approved or fine-tuned to the organisation's needs. Approval of the implementation plan should trigger the next step.

Developing the BIM Champion to Power User level

Before implementation proceeds, the BIM Champion must be able to instil firm-wide confidence in the technical aspects of the BIM approach. This can only be achieved by thorough training and taking sufficient time to ensure that this pivotal individual is able to guide the production of high-quality deliverables through BIM.

The BIM Champion should be tasked with developing a small pilot project to constructional detail. This is because the production of large-scale general arrangement drawings from BIM is relatively straightforward, while most approaches to incorporating detail at smaller scales involve a balance between the addition of ever finer 3D model detail and the embellishment of derived orthogonal views with extensive 2D drafting and annotations. Thus, one of the biggest challenges for new implementations is the development of efficient methods for increasing the detail and information stored in BIM as the project deliverables progress to construction documentation.

On this basis, there should also be a contractual mandate for the BIM implementation consultant to explain how best to combine model and 2D detailing. This would involve a live demonstration of previous models containing convincing examples of useable construction documentation.

Launching an awareness campaign across the business

An early business-wide multi-level awareness campaign should be conducted by the BIM Sponsor and BIM Champion (with the help of external consultants) to promote the business-wide understanding of BIM and its implications for staff. This should never be conducted without first addressing team leaders confidentially in order to gauge their concerns. The firm-wide briefing should explain the corporate vision for BIM at all levels by answering questions like:

- What is BIM in layman's terms?
- What are the corporate reasons for doing

this now? How will this new priority affect employees' ability to fulfil other corporate initiatives?

- How exactly will BIM Level 2 improve the firm's prospects?
- How gradually will the technology and associated processes be introduced?
- What is the schedule for the implementation? Staff names/locations, dates and times.
- Will there be a pilot project?
- In the short term, which sectors and project types will be developed to BIM Level 2?
- Are new roles required? Whose roles will be affected, i.e. what will staff be expected to do? How will the new responsibilities differ from those expected of staff currently?
- What kinds of training are planned and scheduled? Off-site? On-site? Project-based collaboration?
- How will existing work processes and collaborative methods be affected?
- How will new processes be documented?

Change Management

For successful orderly change, careful management is required. To this end, the firm's entire organisational structure should be audited in line with the corporate vision for deriving benefits from BIM. This includes those taking the key role of marketing the benefits of BIM to prospective clients through bids and events.

BIM is not simply a high-powered 3D drawing tool. If used properly, it will affect every aspect of the firm's project data management process. As an example, part of the BIM Protocol used on projects might include an agreement to embed design criteria in the model so that it can be used to develop elemental cost analyses. Normally, these criteria would be added in the form of specification data, requiring the expert input of senior project staff. If this input is not by direct interaction with the model, the team must factor in the time required for technician-level staff to transpose the information from a different format. The time-saving advantages of BIM for cost analysis will not be achieved if considerable time is lost in doing this, or if the

BIM LEVEL 2 ROLE	ACTIVITIES AND AUTHORITY (SEE CHAPTER 3)	POST-HOLDER
Project Delivery Manager/ Project Information Manager. No design related duties.	– Development of Employer's Information Requirements. – Holder of the Master Information Delivery Plan: an aggregated schedule defining who is responsible for developing information deliverables at each project stage. – Establishes the required data standards, level of information and processes for each project work stage. – Receives information into the Information Model in compliance with agreed processes and procedures. – Validates compliance with information requirements and advise on non-compliance – Maintains the Information Model to meet integrity and security standards in compliance with the employer's information requirement. – Manages Common Data Environment processes and procedures for quality, validating compliance with them and advising on non-compliance. – Either an extension of Design Team Leadership or Main Contractor duties. *Authority: Agrees data standards and file formats for Project Outputs*	Either an extension of Design Team Leadership or Main Contractor duties (depending on the project's Work Stage)
Lead Designer	– Coordinated delivery of all design information – Manages information development and information approvals – Confirms design deliverables – Overall lead for managing the configuration of Project Outputs *Authority: Confirms status of information contained in the model and approves for issue within the common data environment; arbitrates and approve design changes proposed to resolve clashes*	Project Lead for overall Design Team Leader
Task Team Manager	– Production of design outputs related to a discipline specific, package based, or time-based task. *Authority: Issues approved design outputs within the common data environment*	Project Architect/ Engineer
Task Information Manager	– Directs the production of task information in compliance with standards and methods and using agreed systems. – Prepares the task information delivery plan. – *Authority: Ensures that information outputs are suitable for issue within the common data environment*	Senior Architectural or Engineering Technician
Interface Manager	– Manages spatial co.ordination on behalf of a task team. – Proposes confinement of structure and services to agreed zones and finds resolutions to coordination clashes. – *Authority: Propose and negotiate resolutions to clashes*	Technical Coordinator (Architect or Engineer)

Table 6.1 BIM roles and responsibilities vis à vis existing staff roles (see PAS-1192-2)

transposition to BIM is only partial. Equally, the benefits of multi-disciplinary coordination in BIM will not be fully realised by a project team that fails to utilise the federated model in their design review sessions.

Remembering to celebrate success

It is important to recognise and celebrate early successes and long-term wins. Recognition by management of exceptional effort (whether by an intranet posting, or a firm-wide email) boosts morale with the same kind of endorsement that should accompany the accomplishment of other major initiatives. It also reassures staff with the knowledge that achieving each objective of the implementation is, indeed, a significant corporate milestone.

ORGANISATIONAL STRUCTURE

What extra roles and resources will we need?

For most design and construction organisations – and for SMEs in particular – there are justifiable concerns about taking on dedicated BIM staff. As a word of reassurance, there is a need to distinguish the required BIM Level 2 role (see PAS-1192-2) from the post-holder likely to perform it.

As can be seen from the table on the previous page, although the BIM roles may appear new and may involve substantial training, they correlate well to the traditional positions identified in the right-hand column.

While larger firms can afford to employ a dedicated BIM Manager, SMEs, in contrast, will have to answer important questions about how these roles can be facilitated by the *organisational* provision of model set-up, administration and technical support.

Building the organisational BIM capability

Most design and construction staff can solve many basic CAD issues without recourse to technical assistance. Typically, if a stand-alone CAD file is corrupted and fails to open, only a single user is affected. By themselves, most users will probably be able to restore the last back-up in a matter of minutes. Restoring an earlier iteration of the multi-user model in BIM requires more care, time and expertise and will affect everyone working on it.

For smaller organisations, the initial cost-effective response to this added expert requirement would be to address BIM support by developing it as a shared organisational capability (see *Human Resources* below).

Handling end-user support

The BIM Champion should field immediate queries about software malfunction and using different functions to develop both interim and formal project deliverables. This is known as first-line support. As a back-up to this role, a contract for telephone support from the software reseller would provide a means of escalating more challenging issues. However, it is important to check the proposed terms and conditions of contract regarding what is accepted as a genuine support question, as opposed to matters that might be declined as arising from a lack of basic end-user training.

Even if a firm has the means to hire a full-time BIM Manager, it makes sense to ensure that, beyond support alone, part of the prospective role is to document BIM project procedures and to produce training materials for all levels in the organisation. Candidates for the position should be able to produce samples of their own clear and consistent BIM documentation and training material.

Setting up BIM projects consistently and publishing documented support responses provides the opportunity for staff to search for answers themselves and, on simpler issues, become less dependent on the BIM Champion. For a while, it may also forestall the need to hire a full-time dedicated BIM Manager.

While this approach has its advantages, the main drawback is that the initially enthusiastic BIM Champion may become disillusioned by the extra workload of combining existing duties with an office-wide BIM support role. At some point, it may be necessary to review staffing policy in order to provide project teams with dedicated BIM support.

ASSETS

Formally, an asset is defined as *'a useful or valuable thing or property owned by a person or company, regarded as having value and available to meet debts, commitment, or legacies.'* Oxford English Dictionary

Assets can range from elements of the physical corporate environment to an organisation's intellectual property. While the role of physical assets is fairly well documented, there are intangible assets that are critical to implementing BIM. Some of these are referred to as Organisational Process Assets and include:

- The processes and procedures for carrying out work
  - Policies
  - Procedures
  - Standard templates
  - General guidelines.
- The corporate knowledge base
  - Historical information
  - Data from previous projects
  - Risk register
  - Lessons learned
  - Stakeholder register.

Part of the role of management is that of an organisational curator. This involves not only cataloguing and archiving standard processes as templates for the entire firm, while reviewing key challenges; it also includes holding events and meetings that publicise the value of these assets to all staff.

For instance, a BIM 'Lessons Learned' session should be held at the end of each project work stage to review the execution plan and to document:

- What went well?
- What didn't go well?
- How might the latter be averted in future?

This should be followed up with a review of existing policies and procedures and an office-wide presentation on how these policies will be amended in the light of these issues.

FINANCIAL STRENGTH

This factor is critical. If an organisation is severely cash-strapped, it must address those challenges with short-term measures to return it to a moderate level of profitability before embarking on its strategic vision for BIM. (It might also prove hard to whip up morale for a new initiative from staff who think that they are one pay day away from redundancy.)

In contrast, financial strength will not only buffer the cost of implementation, it can wield considerable external influence. Despite internal misgivings about the impact of implementing BIM, a wealthy prospective client or supply chain partner that mandates the use of BIM will not be ignored.

HUMAN RESOURCES

While paying due regard to his or her existing workload – and with the assistance of external training development expertise – among the BIM Champion's responsibilities would be to provide expert input on staff development for BIM. This involves imparting advice on the best available learning and training options.

Learning differs from training by imposing greater self-study responsibility on the participant. Part of the BIM role involves developing internal learning modules (ranging from one-page documents to a series of demonstration videos) tailored to the organisation's intended use of BIM. These should cover everything from 'How do I set up a new set of models for a healthcare project?' to 'How can I customise 3D elements of furniture, fixtures and equipment, tag them on drawings and create a schedule of those used in my project?'

It's important to reiterate that the purpose of implementing this tailored training is to achieve the benefits of BIM through organisational upskilling and without necessarily incurring the cost of a full-time dedicated BIM Manager. This approach does incur the cost of course development for which there should be a budget.

If this is outsourced, it will involve the cost of an external expert tasked with developing the tailored training plan. When taken together, this means that, at some point, all organisations wanting to adopt BIM must accept that human resource development costs are involved. That is, expense will be incurred either through developing tailored learning content to establish organisational competence; through hiring a dedicated BIM

Manager to develop procedures, oversee implementation and provide on-going support; or through hiring external expertise to deliver standard training on basic functionality and to devise tailored course modules that ensure staff use BIM in accordance with organisational and project standards.

If you do opt to develop in-house learning content, the next step is to determine the modules that are best suited to each different staff role and the ideal sequence and schedule (i.e. learning path) for working through them. Managers should be tasked with ensuring that those directly reporting to them complete their assigned modules as part of their annually reviewed Personal Development Plans. It is important to emphasise that the firm-wide implementation of this training requires the highest level of managerial support (as described in Chapter 3).

Where possible, use focused training to extend existing roles

The introduction of BIM can often arouse employee anxiety over both its presumed complexity and its potential to eliminate the expertise by which their existing professional experience is distinguished. The reality is that much of the coordination process is still performed in 2D. Moreover, 3D coordination still relies as much on the knowledge and visual scrutiny of experienced technical coordinators as it did before the advent of BIM. So, while checking for clashes can be automated, reviewing the adequacy of safety clearances and maintenance access for services and equipment will involve experienced technical coordinators who can tour the model, check dimensions and add mark-ups of the changes that need to be made.

Instead of commissioning vast swathes of basic software training, what is more appropriate is the gradual introduction of focused training sessions that concentrate on those functions immediately relevant to both existing roles and the extension of them via BIM. For instance, training technical

coordinators on every aspect of using 3D coordination review software (such as Autodesk Navisworks®, Tekla BIMsight® or Bentley Project Navigator®) is nowhere near as effective and efficient as showing them the basics of how these tools can enhance the work that they already do. For example, coordinators should learn how to:

- Tour the model and set up required 3D views before a meeting
- Hide specific elements in order to reveal others that are of more concern
- Section the model
- Measure distances
- Share a snapshot of the model via email.

BIM MANAGER'S ESSENTIAL PROJECT DELIVERY TASK LIST

At this stage, it's worth summarising the essential tasks that the BIM Manager should be expected to undertake:

- Write the BIM Project Execution Plan, having ascertained the following:
  - Project summary
  - Roles, responsibilities and authorities
  - Shared project calendar
  - Common Data Environment (sub-model lists; Levels of Definition; agreed exchange formats)
  - Document and data management
  - Common Origin and Setting Out
  - File/Layer naming convention
  - Information Management.
- In collaboration with the rest of the project team, ensure that specific model development responsibilities are aligned with zonal/disciplinary work-streams as assigned by the Project Architect or Project Manager.
- Establish link between the model(s) and any external databases.
- Establish a folder structure for archiving approved project-specific BIM content; develop an ongoing library of content that is appropriate to each project, especially more complex and customised elements; set up separate folders for end-users to store content in preparation for vetting and further development by the BIM Manager. After this, the content should be added to the main BIM library.
- On large projects, segment the overall design into linked sub-models (named as specified in the BIM Project Execution Plan) for the following aspects of the project: GRID, SITE, SHELL, LANDSCAPE, BASEMENT, INTERIORS, EQUIPMENT, ARCHITECTURE, MASSING, STRUCTURE. This is known as the Volume or Model Division Strategy.
- Propagate all datums and reference points (such as levels, grids and survey coordinates) from the topographical survey drawing into the SITE or GRID model and from there to all other models.
- Run audit on all models in order to maintain prompt file access. Conduct a fortnightly review of:
  - File sizes
  - Warnings per file
  - Extraneous or duplicated elements
  - Use of data structures inside each model (e.g. worksets)
  - Level of model detail and model information.

- Time taken to open and synchronise models across network
- Output from model checking software to ensure compliance with BIM Standards.

- Take remedial action after each audit to improve model organisation and access times. Ensure team is instructed in how they can assist in this task.

- In conjunction with the Project Architect, finalise a deliverables schedule detailed with drawing names, sheet numbering and scales. The list should encompass the BIM Level 2 'data drops'. This becomes the Task Information Delivery Plan.

- Assign drawing sheet responsibilities (to develop, assist and check) in the deliverables schedule.

- Use view controls (e.g. Revit scope boxes) to maintain consistent sheet zones at all levels in the model.

- Produce early sample orthographic drawings and 3D views from the model and submit for review by senior team members, amend in accordance with mark-ups and re-submit for approval as exemplar drawings. Publish the approved drawings to team as exemplars of the intended production information quality for each project stage.

- As far as possible, develop and issue finalised and approved sheet templates with annotation types, key plan, bar scale, north arrow and colour-filled legends that will automate most aspects of the approved production quality.

- Distribute to the modelling team a summarised responsibility matrix for the amending models and drawings to achieve the require output standards. Provide support to team for all changes to the model, including the view control and 2D annotations required to meet presentation standards.

- Export (as required) to agreed alternative formats for issue to the employer and other consultants, facilities management (FM) workshops and visualisation specialists; use screen grabs of 3D views to communicate preferred perspectives to visualisation consultant. Keep a diary regarding difficulties encountered in the export and import of the issued model. Highlight unusual requirements and file translation issues.

- Run information exchange workshops for sub-consultants and/or sub-contractors to facilitate the export of data in the required format from models (see Chapter 10).

- Establish deadlines for sub-consultants and sub-contractors to transmit information in readiness for collating and issuing them formally to the employer.

- Support transitioning the data that comprises the Project Information Model into the employer's Asset Information Model (see Chapter 10).

- Pair experienced technical coordinators with adept BIM coordinators in order to implement agreed coordination changes and resolve interfaces between the models of each discipline (for example, to model agreed revisions of service routes and structural layouts).

- Review the agenda in advance of design team meetings, and prepare drawings and corresponding 3D views of the model in readiness for the issues to be raised.
  - In BIM coordination software (e.g Autodesk Navisworks®), prepare major sections through the combined 3D model in order to help verify adequate coordination between several sub-models.
  - Review opportunities for using BIM to generate 3D presentation visuals, 4D animations and 5D quantities.

CONCLUSION

There are significant implications for adopting BIM Level 2 for the first time. It is important to plan the implementation carefully and address the impact on the whole organisation.

These are summarised in terms of:

- Organisational culture
- Management
- Organisational structure
- Assets
- Financial strength
- Human resources.

We have seen how each of these will affect how BIM is deployed. The choice of whether internal expertise is developed by informal internal effort, a dedicated manager or external expertise is a critical one. If you do opt for a dedicated manager, the above task list should be useful in establishing the scope of required duties.

---

[1] Chatman, J. A., & Eunyoung Cha, S. (2003). Leading by leveraging culture. California Management Review , 45 , 1934; Kerr, J., & Slocum, J. W., Jr. (2005). Managing corporate culture through reward systems. Academy of Management Executive , 19 , 130138.

07

BIM AND CONTRACTS
BY PROFESSOR DAVID MOSEY

INTRODUCTION

In this chapter we will look at the contractual and legal implications of BIM for project team members. The Government Construction Clients Group suggested in March 2011 that *'Little change is required in the fundamental building blocks of copyright law, contracts or insurance to facilitate working at Level 2 of BIM maturity.'* [1] We will examine the extent to which project teams implementing BIM should rely on this assessment.

The key coverage of this chapter is as follows;
- How does BIM affect contractual duties of care?
- How is BIM dealt with in standard form construction contracts and consultant appointments?
- How does the CIC BIM Protocol work?
- BIM and Contracts: The key issues
- Does BIM affect advice on procurement models?
- Lessons Learned from Cookham Wood Case Study.

HOW DOES BIM AFFECT CONTRACTUAL DUTIES OF CARE?

BIM is a set of systems that should facilitate and support agreed activities of design, costing, programming, project management, construction and post-completion operation. Adopting BIM does not automatically affect the duties of care agreed under contract or imposed by law in respect of those activities. However, the way that BIM increases data exchange and its dependence on computer software programmes can influence legal liability, while the aspirations of BIM users to improve collaboration and efficiency need to be framed within appropriate and insurable legal commitments.

The duty of a consultant to use *'reasonable skill and care'* in creating a design,[2] and its duty to produce a design that is buildable,[3] should not be affected by the adoption of BIM. Likewise, the risk of raising a consultant's duty of care to *'fitness for purpose'* in

respect of what a design will achieve – and the consequent concern that this will not be supported by professional indemnity insurance – should not occur by reason of adopting BIM. In either case, any change to the designer consultant's duty of care occurs only by agreement of additional contractual commitments.[4]

Meanwhile, the implied design duty of *'fitness for purpose'* that is the starting point for a design and build contractor,[5] or for the supplier or manufacturer of a product,[6] should also not be affected by adoption of BIM and can only be reduced by a clear provision of the type found in most building contracts.[7]

The following is worth keeping in mind when advising a client on the adoption of BIM for the first time: *'Architects who are venturing into the untried or little tried would be wise to warn their clients specifically of what they are doing and to obtain their express approval.'*

SO WHAT HAS BEEN CHANGED BY BIM?

Reasonable skill and care

The following factors are useful when assessing *'reasonable skill and care'* in the world of BIM:

- In its approach to BIM a consultant is expected *'not to lag behind other ordinarily assiduous and intelligent members of his profession in knowledge of the new advances, discoveries and developments in his field'.* [9] This means keeping up with the profession, firstly in advising on the benefits and risks of adopting BIM, and secondly in applying BIM to the design process and to related costing, programming and project management services.

- The professional knowledge and practices relating to BIM are continually evolving. A consultant falling behind the advance of BIM is entitled to claim that it applied *'the state of the art'* at the time of giving its advice, although this defence will be judged by reference to the guidance and publications available to the profession as a whole at that time. [10]

- Where there is a contractual obligation to comply with the Construction (Design and Management) Regulations 2015, the duty of care in relation to BIM may also be assessed in terms of its impact on a designer's duty when *'preparing or modifying a design'* to *'eliminate, so far as is reasonably practical, foreseeable risks to the health and safety of any person',* or otherwise to reduce or control those risks, and *'to take all reasonable steps to provide, with the design, sufficient information about the design, construction or maintenance of the structure to adequately assist the client, other designers and contractors to comply with their duties.'* [11]

Duty to review designs

As regards a designer's duty to review and check its own designs and those of other designers at each stage of BIM model development:

- Increased access to BIM data emerging throughout the life of a project could increase the likelihood that a designer has become aware, or should become aware, of the need to reconsider an earlier design. [12]

- Increased access through BIM to other team members' designs could affect a designer's duty to warn of errors or problems it notices in another team member's work. [13]

Limits of design liability

In establishing the limits of design liability under BIM:

- The transparency of BIM models and the way that BIM models fit together should assist in identifying more precisely who does what design and where each team member's design liability starts and stops.

- This should clarify the right of designers to rely on other team members' earlier, simultaneous or later design contributions.

BIM Information Manager

As to the liability of the BIM Information Manager and the ability of other consultants to rely on the BIM Information Manager:

- Both depend firstly on clarifying exactly what the BIM Information Manager does, noting for example CIC Protocol guidance: *'The Information Manager has no design related duties.'* [14]

- The ability to rely on the BIM Information Manager as a specialist depends in part on the designer acting reasonably in this reliance. [15]

HOW IS BIM DEALT WITH IN STANDARD FORM CONSTRUCTION CONTRACTS AND CONSULTANT APPOINTMENTS?

KEY POINTS

Before we look at the terms and conditions of standard forms, the place to start is in the scope of a contractor's brief or a consultant's schedule of services. The following key points should be checked:

- Does the contract contain a clear set of obligations as to how the consultant or contractor will be expected to implement BIM, including for example whether this will start with the project procurement process and continue into post-completion operation?
- Are there clear statements of the consultants or contractor's promised BIM experience and expertise?
- Is it made clear what effect the use of BIM will have on the consultant's or contractor's specific duties in respect of design, costing, programming, project management and construction?
- Do all parties understand who will be BIM Information Manager, what duties this role will comprise and how these duties will interface with those of the design lead and the project manager so as to avoid gaps or duplications? [16]

STANDARD FORMS

As regards terms and conditions relating to BIM, the standard form building contracts, consultant appointments and related guidance have so far used a light touch. This reflects the fact that BIM does not necessarily change how standard forms allocate risk and liability or how they deal with the project processes.

Some standard form building contracts expressly mention BIM, showing that the relevant drafting body has taken BIM into account. Examples are the JCT *'Public Sector Supplement'*,[17] PPC2000 *'Appendix 10'*,[18] and several clauses in the CIoB *'Complex Projects Form'*.[19] Some standard forms mention their approach to BIM only in guidance documents, for example *'How to use BIM with NEC3 Contracts'*.[20] Meanwhile, certain standard form building contracts such as FIDIC are silent on BIM, which leaves uncertainty for the user as to whether BIM has yet been taken into account by the drafting bodies. Most standard form consultant appointments are also silent on BIM, although some refer in their guidance to the *'CIC BIM Protocol'* described below.

However, to look for a mention of BIM in a contract is not the most effective way of determining a contract's suitability to support the adoption of BIM in practice. Instead, it is better to look at how the contract deals with the key issues affected by BIM. These issues are examined below.

It is also important to look at whether there is consistency on these issues as between the building contract, all consultant appointments and also any sub-contracts and supply agreements that govern a design contribution. For example, there are complete and consistent sets of NEC3 and PPC2000 contract forms, but JCT offers no consultant appointment except for public sector projects [21] and in those cases it will be necessary to align all other consultant forms with the JCT treatment of BIM. One way of ensuring consistency in the contractual treatment of BIM was the publication in 2013 of the 'CIC BIM Protocol', and this is what we will examine next.

HOW DOES THE CIC BIM PROTOCOL WORK?

The CIC BIM Protocol is a supplementary contract document signed, in addition to each consultant agreement or building contract, by each project team member – including every consultant, the main contractor and any sub-contractors and suppliers who make design contributions. In the event of conflict or discrepancy, it overrides the consultant appointment or building contract (Clause 2.2).

LICENSING OF MODELS

The provisions and guidance of the CIC BIM Protocol propose a reasonably balanced approach to the licensing of BIM models, including:

- Grant of a non-exclusive licence for the client to transmit, copy and use models for the agreed project-related purposes for which they were prepared (Clause 6.3).
- The right for the client to grant equivalent sub-licences and for team members to grant equivalent sub-sub-licences (Clauses 6.3, 6.6, 6.7).

- Exclusion of the right to amend models except for agreed purposes (Clause 6.5.1) and exclusion of the right to reproduce models for the purpose of project extensions (Clause 6.5.2).
- Mutual obligations on the client and project team members to procure licences as required to meet their agreed licence obligations under the protocol (Clauses 6.9, 6.10).

LIMITS OF LIABILITY

The protocol also includes the following limits on a project team member's liability:

- No warranty as to the integrity of electronic data transmission, and no liability for corruption or alteration occurring after transmission (Clause 5).
- Cross-reference to support any right to revoke or suspend a licence to use models in the event of non-payment (Clause 6.4).
- No liability for the modification, amendment, transmission, copying or use of BIM models other than for agreed purposes (Clause 7).

APPENDICES

The Appendices to the CIC BIM Protocol comprise important practical documents, namely:

- Appendix 1: The *'Model Production and Delivery Table',* which sets out the *'Levels of Detail'* to be achieved in respect of each BIM model by each project team member at each stage.
- Appendix 2: Details of the BIM Information Manager's role, and of the *'Employer's Information Requirements'* regarding the *"Common Data Environment"* created through BIM, including agreed software and formats plus cross-reference to the BIM *'Execution Plan'* and related project procedures.

These documents need to be integrated with the consultant services schedules, the contractor's brief and the project programme.

DUTY OF CARE

The obligation on project team members to produce models in accordance with agreed Levels of Detail specified in the Model Production and Delivery Table is limited to *'reasonable endeavours',* a lower duty of care than the accepted standard of *'reasonable skill and care'* (Clause 4). In addition, a team member's compliance with the Model Production and Delivery Table and the Information Requirements is stated to be *'subject to events outside its reasonable control'* (Clause 4), a generic exception which overrides the detailed provisions for extension of time contained in all standard form building contracts.

CLIENT CONCERNS

Some of the above provisions dilute what a client would expect as commercial norms, and anyone recommending the CIC BIM Protocol should make very clear its potential impact on client rights.

The absolute obligation on the client to secure protocols in substantially the same form from all other project team members, and to update the Information Requirements and the Model Production and Delivery Table (Clause 3), should also be made clear to the client before the CIC BIM Protocol is adopted.

BIM AND CONTRACTS: THE KEY ISSUES

There are practical measures by which project teams can use contracts to get the best out of BIM while not exposing themselves to additional liability, and these are set out below. Some of these issues are dealt with (to varying degrees) in existing standard form contracts; others need additional attention, particularly to ensure consistency as to how they are addressed in consultant appointments and building contracts. In all cases, it will be important for advisers on a project using BIM to check how these issues are dealt with in the contractual provisions and procedures before making a recommendation.

CONTRACTUAL STATUS OF MODEL PRODUCTION AND DELIVERY TABLE

BIM provides clarity as to the Level of Detail in each model at each stage of a project, and requires that consultant appointments and building contracts reflect that clarity in deadlines setting out the agreed sequence of model production, delivery, comment and approval. There should be a contractual commitment by all team members:

* To produce and deliver their BIM models to the agreed Level of Detail by agreed deadlines at each stage
* To provide comments and approvals by agreed deadlines at each stage
* To specify matters that may prevent agreed deadlines being met.

Certain standard form building contracts provide documents that could be linked to or embody the Model Production and Delivery Table, for example:

* The JCT *Information Release Schedule,*[22] although this only commits the main contractor under the JCT 20111 building contracts, with no corresponding commitment in the JCT Consultant Appointment (Public Sector).
* The NEC *Key Dates Schedule,*[23] which appears both in the NEC Building Contract and in the NEC Professional Services Contract.
* The PPC2000 *Partnering Timetable and Project Timetable*[24] which, under the PPC multi-party structure, mutually commits the main contractor and all consultants to agreed deadlines.

MECHANISMS TO ACHIEVE COLLABORATION AND CONSENSUS

BIM is often described as collaborative, and clearly creates significant opportunities for team members to work collaboratively, but without additional discussions this may go no further than agreed arrangements for sharing BIM data and expecting timely feedback. These can be dealt with in the agreement of deadlines for model production, delivery, comment and approval as described in above.

If collaboration through BIM is intended also to describe the culture of the project and the way that team members assist each other, then this needs clarification in the contract terms so that there is no room for misunderstanding or opting out. For example, a forum for clash detection, early warning and risk management is described in the next section. Other contract provisions that support a collaborative culture include:

* Direct mutual agreement to act in *'good faith'* or otherwise in a collaborative manner
* Direct mutual commitment to agreed objectives.

These appear, for example, in the following standard forms:

* In the JCT forms, a *'good faith'* provision appears in the optional Appendix 8 to the 2011 building contracts – but there is no equivalent commitment in the JCT Consultant Agreement (Public Sector).
* In the JCT forms, mutual direct commitments to agreed objectives appear only in the *'JCT Constructing Excellence Project Agreement'.*
* In NEC3, a *'good faith'* provision is given in Clause 10.1 of all building contracts and the consultant appointment form.
* In NEC3, no mutual direct commitments are given, as these are expressly excluded in *NEC3 Partnering Option X12.*
* In PPC2000, a *'good faith'* provision is included in Clause 1.3 of the PPC2000 Partnering Terms.
* In PPC2000, the multi-party structure creates mutual direct commitments between the client, all consultants, the main contractor and key sub-contractors.

CLASH DETECTION, EARLY WARNING AND RISK MANAGEMENT

BIM enables design inconsistencies to be revealed through clash detection, but for BIM to enable collaborative working, there needs to be a contractual mechanism establishing what team members do when clashes are detected and notified. This should comprise a forum tasked with seeking a constructive solution. Although the JCT forms do not provide for such forums, both NEC Option X 12[25] and PPC2000[26] provide for such *'Core Groups.'*

INTELLECTUAL PROPERTY LICENCES

Intellectual property rights should not need different protections by virtue of appearing in BIM models. For example, existing statutory copyright protection covers graphic and non-graphic design work plus *'computer programmes'* and *'preparatory design material for a computer programmes'*, and arguably does not need clarification to extend to BIM models. [27]

However, it is important to spell out that athough the CIC Protocol offers a balanced approach to the licensing of BIM models, it creates an additional burden on the client by making it the contractual gatekeeper of all model licences, leaving project team members without direct remedies in the event of breach of each other's licences. The multi-party structure of the PPC2000 contract solves these problems by creating direct licences and mutual indemnities between all the project team members who sign it.

LIABILITY FOR CORRUPTION OF DATA

It is worrying that the CIC BIM Protocol excludes any warranty as to the integrity of electronic data delivered, and also excludes liability in respect of any corruption or amendment of data after transmission. This places all risks with the client, and does not, for example, require project team members to apportion any liability to the BIM software providers. By contrast, there are no equivalent exclusions in the JCT, NEC3 or PPC2000 standard form building contracts.

LINKS BETWEEN DESIGN, CONSTRUCTION AND OPERATION

The benefits of BIM should extend long beyond completion of a capital project, if it is used to create accessible data that supports interactive operation and maintenance systems in place of traditional *'O and M'* manuals. For example, the UK Government's *'Soft landings'* initiative includes trials of new project team contractual commitments, supported by BIM, which extend beyond the typical defects liability period.

Standard contract forms can link the capital and operational phases of a project, and the JCT, NEC and PPC contract suites all offer compatible *'term'* contract forms. However, the development of contract models that help to fulfil the operational potential of BIM data also depends on the adoption of procurement models which invite the market to submit whole-life asset management proposals.

Closer integration of design, construction and operation phases in the life of a built asset forms part of the UK Government's approach to BIM level 3. For example, *'Digital Built Britain'* includes proposals for the *'Development of BIM and asset data enabled FM and AM Contracts'* [28] (see Chapter 4).

DOES BIM AFFECT ADVICE ON PROCUREMENT MODELS?

Traditionally, advice on selection of a procurement model has focussed only on identifying which team member or members are responsible for design, and on how to transfer design and construction risk away from the client. The only procurement options that also focus on the timing of each team member's appointment have involved fragmentation of these responsibilities through the separate appointments of individual specialist contractors.

So, if BIM is intended to support a collaborative approach, can a new procurement model be devised that obtains BIM model contributions from the main contractor and from specialist contractors without fragmenting the warranties relied on by the client?

Early contractor and supplier design input has been advocated for many years, for example by the ICE (as quoted in *'Accelerating Change'*), which states, *'Designers must involve the contractors, specialist subcontractors and key manufacturers as soon as possible. In order to interpret and develop a functional brief it is essential that designers (including specialist subcontractors and key manufacturers) are able to get close to clients.'* [29]

While early contractor involvement has been devised ad hoc by individual project teams and although it is a model embedded in the PPC2000 contract form, the UK Government introduced the first formal assessment of its merits under a *'Trial Projects'* programme pursuant to their 2011 *'Government Construction Strategy'*. Meanwhile, the Royal Institute of British Architects restructured its *'2013 Plan of Work'* to identify design work stages that can be led by an early appointed main contractor and its specialist supply chain, integrated as members of a single design team.[30]

The Government's *'Two Stage Open Book'* procurement model was adopted on Trial Projects combining early contractor involvement with BIM. This creates a single project team, including the main contractor, which is appointed early under a conditional contract and a binding timetable describing how they will work together through BIM to develop designs, agree costs and reduce risks ahead of the client approving start on site.[31]

The results achieved through the Government's Trial Projects are set out in online guidance which describes the prerequisites, processes and techniques for successful early contractor involvement, and the measurable benefits this can help to achieve, particularly when implemented in conjunction with BIM.[32] These benefits include audited savings of up to 20 per cent, greater cost and time transparency, improved quality control and risk management, improved opportunities for small to medium enterprises and other local/regional businesses, and greater employment and skills commitments.

We will next examine the first detailed Government case study of BIM combined with *'Two Stage Open Book'* in order to consider what lessons it offers when advising on the best procurement options to adopt in conjunction with BIM.

LESSONS LEARNED FROM THE COOKHAM WOOD CASE STUDY

For the team that delivered the Cookham Wood Trial Project, a combination of early contractor involvement, collaborative working and BIM was integral to the results achieved. BIM Level 2 models were used in the brief issued to prospective main contractors, and were developed by bidders as part of their proposals for project team selection. Interserve Construction were appointed as main contractor and lead designer, bringing with them Arup as consulting engineers, EMCOR as mechanical and electrical specialists, and SCC as precast volumetric cell providers. HLN Architects were the Ministry of Justice's (MoJ) appointed designer and technical assessor.

SAVINGS AND IMPROVED VALUE ACHIEVED USING BIM

The Cookham Wood Trial Project case study, which was independently audited, attributed significant improved value to 'Two Stage Open Book' and BIM. These included 20 per cent agreed savings, namely a cost of £2,332 per square metre against a baseline benchmark of £2,910 per square metre. For example, Interserve and its tier 2 specialist subcontractor SCC submitted a *'precast volumetric cell'* proposal in response to the MoJ brief; this was developed through BIM by the wider design team and led to a time saving of six weeks and a saving in overheads of £85,000.[33]

Other innovations driven by 'Two Stage Open Book' and BIM included:

- The use of solid precast floor slabs in place of pre-stressed floor slabs, resulting in a time saving of 12 days.
- The creation of *'indestructible'* lighting in the education block through a bespoke solution proposed by EMCOR that also created a significant cost saving.
- Development by Arup and EMCOR of service ducts and cell risers that could be serviced more quickly and reliably by repair and maintenance engineers.[34]

BIM EXECUTION PLAN AND CORE GROUP

Interserve prepared a BIM Execution Plan linked to a series of agreed deadlines in relation to the preconstruction phase of the project.[35] By this means, specified Construction Operations Building Information Exchange (COBie) data drops and related activities were supported by clear contractual obligations, including peer group pressure under the governance of named individuals comprising the *'Core Group'*. Core Group members met whenever required to approve design development proposals and to resolve questions and problems arising from clash detection, in each case deciding on courses of action by unanimous agreement of all members present.[36] This group worked alongside the design team, who were tasked with the development, coordination and exchange of information through the BIM models.

MUTUAL RELIANCE AND CLASH DETECTION

Each team member agreed to be responsible for errors, omissions and discrepancies in the BIM models it prepared or contributed to, *'except to the extent of its reliance (if stated in such Partnering Documents) on any contribution or information provided by any one or more other Partnering Team members'*.[37] As the sequence and nature of each contribution was spelled out, each team member was contractually entitled to rely on all earlier designs, and was made aware of which partners would rely on the completeness, accuracy and timeliness of that member's contributions.

The team members agreed to warn each other *'of any error, omission or discrepancy of which they become aware and (within the scope of their agreed roles, expertise and responsibilities) to put forward proposals to resolve any such error, omission or discrepancy fairly and constructively within the Partnering Team without adversely affecting the agreed cost or time for completion or quality of the project'*.[38] This clause underpinned the commitment of all parties to BIM clash detection and to the notification of pragmatic

solutions. It helped to establish that no team member would, by notifying a warning of clash detection and a proposal to resolve it, be charged with any additional responsibilities beyond those already within its agreed contractual role and expertise.

INTELLECTUAL PROPERTY LICENCES

Under the multi-party structure, a set of mutual intellectual property licences were directly entered into between all team members *'for any purpose relating to the completion of the Project and (only in regard to the Client) the Operation of the Project'*.[39] As regards liability arising from the licensing of intellectual property rights, the liability of team members was excluded *'for the use of any design or document that it prepares for any purpose other than that for which it was agreed to be prepared as stated in, or reasonably inferred from, the Partnering Documents'*.[40]

CONCLUSION

This chapter has demonstrated how to secure contractual protections for all project team members by looking for specific provisions and processes that support BIM. It has shown how integrated collaborative contracts and early contractor involvement can help BIM to fulfil its potential. It has also explained the contract systems used to deliver savings and other improved value on the Cookham Wood Trial Project.

[1] Government Construction Client Group BIM Working Party Strategy Paper, March 2011: www.bimtaskgroup.org, paragraph 5.2
[2] *George Hawkins v Chrysler (UK)* (1986) 38 BLR 36
[3] *EDAC v Moss* (1984) 2 Con LR 1
[4] *Greaves & Co (Contractors) v Baynham Meikle* (1975) I WLR 1095
[5] *Viking Grain Storage v T H White Installations* (1985) 33 BLR 103
[6] Sale of Goods Act 1979, 1994, Section 14(3)
[7] For example JCT DB (2011), Clause 2.17.1; NEC3 Option X15; PPC2000 Clause 22.1
[8] *Victoria University of Manchester v Hugh Wilson and Lewis Womersley* (1984) 1 Const LJ 162
[9] *Ekkerslie v Binnie* (1988) 18 Con LR 1(CA)
[10] *Wimpey Construction UK v Poole* (1984) 2 Lloyds Rep 499
[11] The Construction (Design and Management) Regulations 2015, Regulation 9
[12] *Samuel Payne v John Setchell* (2002) BLR 489 (TCC)
[13] *Tesco v Norman Hitchcox Partnership* (1997) 56 Con LR 42. *Murphy & Sons v Johnston Precast* (2008) EWHC 3104 (TCC)
[14] CIC BIM Protocol Guidance, Note 4
[15] *Cooperative Group v John Allen* (2010) EWHC 2300 (TCC)
[16] See for example PAS1192-2 (2013)
[17] JCT Public Sector Supplement (2011)
[18] PPC2000 Standard Form of Contract for Project Partnering, amended 2013, Association of Consultant Architects and the Association for Consultancy and Engineering
[19] Chartered Institute of Building, Complex Projects Contract (2013)
[20] *How to use BIM with NEC3 Contracts* (2013)

21 JCT Consultancy Agreement (Public Sector) (2011)

23 JCT SBC/Q (2011), Clause 2.11

24 PPC2000, Clauses 6.1 and 6.5

25 NEC3 Option X12: Partnering, Clause X12.2 and X12.3

26 PPC2000, Clause 3

27 Copyright Designs and Patents Act 1988, Section 3(1)

28 Digital Built Britain, Level 3 Building Information Modelling – Strategic Plan (February 2015)

29 Strategic Forum for Construction, Accelerating Change (2002), Section 26: *www.strategicforum.org.uk*

30 *www.architecture.com/TheRIBA/AboutUs/Professionalsupport/RIBAOutlinePlanofWork2013*

31 *www.gov.uk/government/collections/new-models-of-construction-procurement*

32 'Project Procurement and Delivery Guidance Using Two Stage Open Book and Supply Chain Collaboration', King's College London Centre of Construction Law and the UK Cabinet Office: *www.gov.uk/government/publications/two-stage-open-book*

33 Cookham Wood Trial Project Case Study, n.24, p.3

34 Cookham Wood Trial Project Case Study, n.24, pp.3–4

35 PPC2000, Clauses 6.1 and 6.5 (Partnering Timetable and Project Timetable) and model Partnering Timetable (Appendix 6)

36 PPC2000, Clauses 3.3 (Core Group and members), 3.4 (Responsibility for Core Group members), 3.5 (Core Group meetings) and 3.6 (Core Group decisions)

37 PPC2000, Clause 2.4 (Responsibility for Partnering Documents)

38 PPC2000, Clause 2.5 (Partnering Documents complementary)

39 PPC2000, Clause 9.2 (Licence to copy and use)

40 PPC2000, Clause 9.3 (Liability for use of designs and documents)

08

BIM COLLABORATION AND WORKING WITHIN THE COMMON DATA ENVIRONMENT

INTRODUCTION

While the focus of the Government BIM Strategy has been on formal 'data drops' for gateway reviews and asset information, there is an ongoing need for project team members to improve their collaboration by regularly sharing informal 'work in progress' information with each other. This chapter highlights the importance to team collaboration of using BIM effectively in the Common Data Environment.

The key coverage in this chapter is as follows:
- The risks of information model sharing in the CDE
- Open BIM workflows
- Value and design fixity in BIM
- Capturing design options in BIM
- Automatic design verification in BIM.

THE RISKS OF INFORMATION MODEL SHARING IN THE CDE

The Common Data Environment (CDE) was described in Chapter 2 as *'a single source of information for any given project, used to collect, manage and disseminate all relevant approved project documents for multi-disciplinary teams in a managed process'*. Given that the multi-disciplinary team may be geographically dispersed, it makes sense for this requirement to be fulfilled by an online data repository.

The diagram below indicates the four major categories of information exchanged through the CDE: **Work in Progress**, **Shared, Published Documentation** (as approved by the client) and **Archive** (the last is ultimately verified to be 'as-built' at hand-over).

The Common Data Environment should be able to provide the following:
- Authentication of all personnel who use the system and are designated to exchange information through it on behalf of their respective project team members.

- A consistently applied file naming convention capable of adequately distinguishing all revisions to the model files, drawings and data extracted from them.
- Form-based user interface for assigning properties that indicate the purpose for which each model is being issued.
- An 'audit trail' of the file exchange sequence that indicates the progression of model development throughout the design and construction process.
- Verification of which revision of each model is to be used in conjunction with others.
- Assurance that project members are working with the most recently approved versions of each other's models and issued data.

Design data is typically shared among project team members far more regularly than it is issued to the client for approval. The purpose of the Shared section of the Common Data Environment is to ensure that multi-disciplinary design proposals and model changes are continuously collected and correctly disseminated with recipients notified.

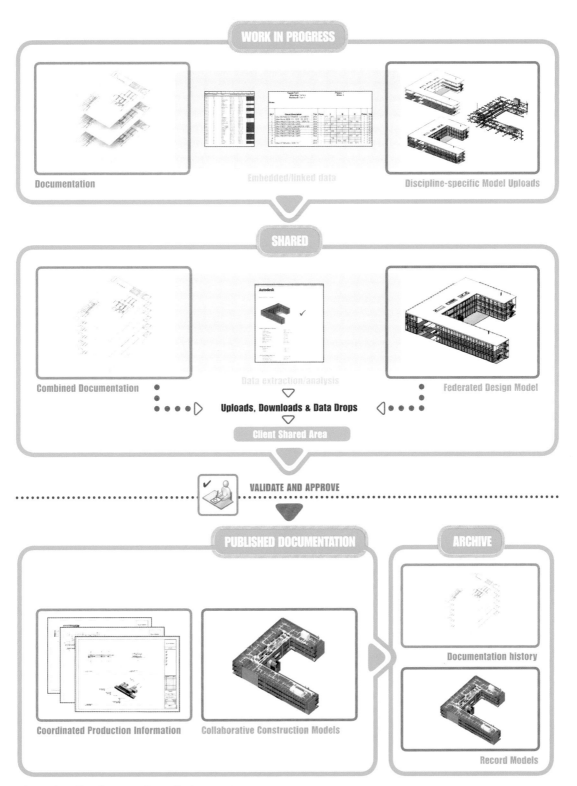

Figure 8.1 The Common Data Environment

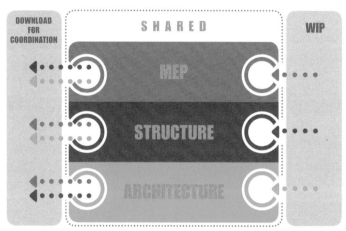

Figure 8.2 Informal information exchanges - Work-in-progress (WIP) is verified by each discipline and uploaded for coordination through the Common Data Environment

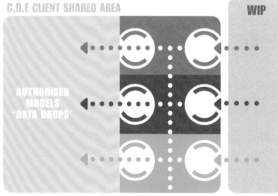

Figure 8.3 Formal 'data drops' as agreed in BEP, Lead Designer/ Main Contractor coordinate and verify project models and data before scheduled submission for approval through the Client Shared Area of the Common Data Environment

Despite best intentions, the relative ease and informality of these information exchanges can lead to complacency. Whereas drawing changes will be clearly identified through revision clouds and notes, the annotation of significant revisions to shared models is not nearly as commonplace.

Applying change control to the model is important because the model is the chief means of communicating definitive design consensus in BIM Level 2. The CIC BIM Protocol establishes that in cases of discrepancies between the model and information extracted from it (such as drawings and schedules), the model should normally take precedence.

OPEN BIM WORKFLOWS

When the model is shared through the CDE with the aim of achieving consensus collaboratively, there is often a need to initiate a discussion about a specific design issue or problem and associate it with specific elements stored in the model.

The exchange of BIM data in proprietary formats that are incompatible with each other can actually hinder the fluidity of communication between project participants. As a means of overcoming this incompatibility, there is an industry-wide non-proprietary data structure for defining 3D BIM objects, called Industry Foundation Classes (IFC). Its ongoing development was the responsibility of the former Industry Alliance for Interoperability (IAI), which when it was founded in 1994 as a consortium comprising the largest CAD software vendors and a number of major US building industry firms. Over the next two decades, the IAI expanded globally into what is now known as buildingSMART International.

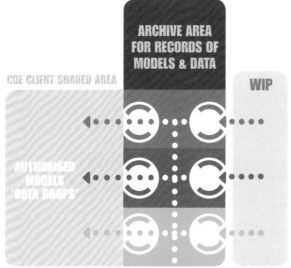

Alongside IFC development, the BIM Collaboration Format (BCF) evolved as an additional non-proprietary, open data standard for communicating design and construction issues via the 3D model. Although it was introduced by Solibri, Inc. and Tekla Corporation in 2009, there are now a range of BCF applications that are add-ons to most industry-leading BIM design creation programs.

As shown in fig.8.5 below, the BCF issue file includes a description of the issue itself, links to the specific BIM elements involved, and the key model view in which recipients can locate the issue.

Figure 8.4 Maintaining project history: At key milestones, project models and data are transferred to the Archive Area in the Common Data Environment

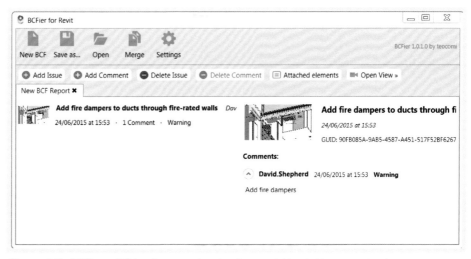

Figure 8.5 BCFier: a BIM software extension for model-based issue capture[i]

To highlight an issue in the model using BCF, the user selects one or more elements in a 3D view and clicks on the 'Add Issue' button. The resulting dialog box will launch the PC's standard picture editor for marking up a small image capture of the chosen model view. Furthermore, several of these issues can be captured and compressed into a single BCF file (*.bcfzip) which can be distributed via the Common Data Environment to other members of the project team for comment.

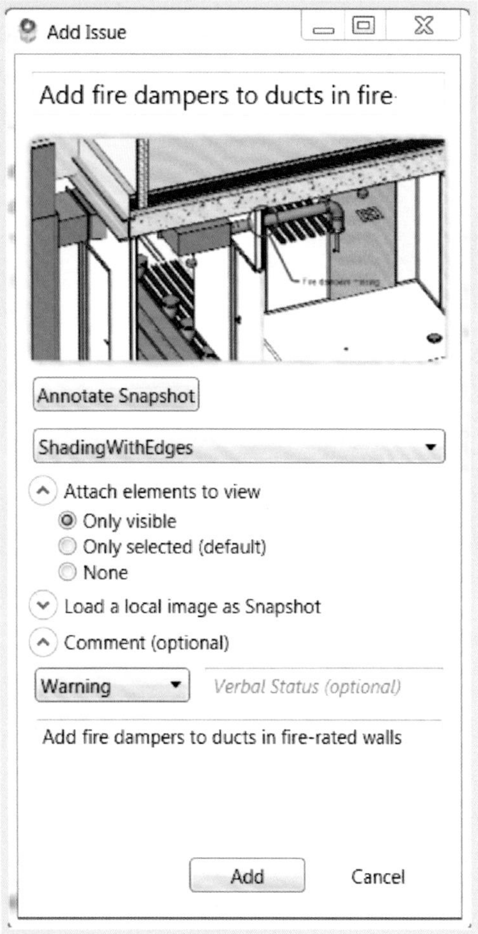

The recipient opens the issued model and compressed BCF Report file. Clicking on any of the listed items will not only display the marked up image, but also open the model in the intended model view and select the associated model elements.

CREATING A 'READ-ONLY' MODEL SNAPSHOT

As shown below, the BIM Collaboration File correlates each issue to its associated model elements by means of the global unique IDs (GuIDs) that distinguish every object exported to IFC.

Given the possibility that the authored model might inadvertently be updated by the recipient, it is often better to export the static IFC model that relates specifically to the issues identified in the BIM Collaboration File. There are several software applications for opening and walking through IFC files in 3D, including Solibri Model Checker®, Tekla BIMSight® and Autodesk Navisworks®. A range of add-on applications have been developed for these tools, enabling users to review issues recorded in the BIM Collaboration File in conjunction with the IFC model.

ASSIGNING AND NOTIFYING OF MODEL STATUS

Those involved in developing the BIM Project Execution Plan for a given project should prioritise the implementation of form-based mechanisms for classifying and notifying recipients of the overall purpose for which different model revisions were intended. This

Figure 8.6 Adding an issue in BCF

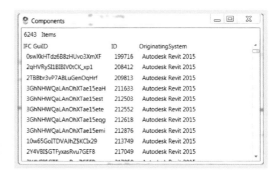

Figure 8.7 List of IFC elements correlated to a particular BCF issue

and other descriptive information about each model are known as meta data.

PAS-1192 provides a list of abbreviations, called status codes, that should be used as meta data to signify the purpose and quality of issued information.

REVIEW ONLY MODEL REVISIONS

Often, work-in-progress models are issued as an exploration of a design concept, and for review only, rather than for definitive design coordination. As described in Chapter 3, model revision file naming would be expected to adhere to an industry-standard convention, such as BS-1192. In accordance with the latter, before issuing 'review only' revisions, file name suffixes should be changed from P01, P02 to R01, R02, etc.

On receipt, the file should be downloaded to a date-stamped sub-folder on the recipient firm's server where the project's incoming files are stored. The file should not be opened directly, as it is a record of the issued model. Instead, it should be copied into an appropriate review folder and opened as a standalone file. While any links to other models must be reloaded, under no circumstances should the previously accepted model revision be overwritten until a new formal P revision is issued.

VALUE AND DESIGN FIXITY IN BIM

Design fixity is attained through what is known as 'Last Responsible Moment' (LRM) decision-making. The LRM is that team review decision-point beyond which the cost of delay outweighs the benefit of delay.

Fixity is attained on a design issue relating to specific elements when there is sufficient consensus among key decision–makers for the project to progress. It is not the same as 'design freeze', since the latter establishes constraints on the scope of further design development. Nevertheless, fixity does provide an agreed basis for making and communicating decisions.

Table 3 – Status codes in the CDE

Status	Description
Work in Progress (WIP)	
S0	Initial status or WIP Master document index of file identifiers uploaded into the extranet.
Shared	
S1	Issued for co-ordination The file is available to be "shared" and used by other disciplines as a background for their information.
S2	Issued for information
S3	Issued for internal review and comment
S4	Issued for construction approval
S5	Issued for manufacture
S6	Issued for PIM authorization (Information Exchanges 1-3)
S7	Issued for AIM authorization (Information Exchange 6)
D1	Issued for costing
D2	Issued for tender
D3	Issued for contractor design
D4	Issued for manufacture/procurement
AM	As maintained
Published documentation	
A	Issued for construction
B	Partially signed-off: For construction with minor comments from the client. All minor comments should be indicated by the insertion of a cloud and a statement of "in abeyance" until the comment is resolved, then resubmitted for full authorization.
AB	As-built handover documentation, PDF, native models, COBie, etc.

Figure 8.8 Status Codes in the CDE (PAS-1192-2)[2]

DOCUMENT NUMBER								REVISION
Field 1	Field 2	Field 3	Field 4	Field 5	Field 6	Field 7	Field 8	
ABC	SRV	02	M3	ZZ	S	21	0001	R01
Project	Originator	Zone	Type	Level	Role	Element	Sequential Number	Revision

Figure 8.9 Review document numbering example[3]

The 'Last Responsible Moment' for any issue is a decision for the Project Manager to make, but it will be informed by several factors, including the required lead-time for developing and issuing documentation. Since awaiting further expert input indefinitely is not a viable option, the design team must commit to a decision at that LRM or begin to lose money.

In these situations, the model is ideal for quickly disseminating the team's consensus on design issues across the entire project. The publishing of an interim federated model (with fully annotated changes) to all project members will ensure that each discipline promptly institutes coordinated changes in respect of any aspect of design fixity that affects them.

For example, consider the design and procurement process for a specific construction work package, such as groundwater and drainage. The design would need to undergo specialist technical and cost review before it is formally issued to the main contractor. Although the team might want to postpone issuing the design to ensure that it fully incorporates belated specialist input from the appointed subcontractor, further delay might compromise the overall project deadline and incur severe penalties. At that point, it would be better to issue coordinated data that represents the design team's consensus on the best information to date, so that the contractor can maintain progress on the project. That data would be issued provisionally on the understanding that it still requires a measure of revision in the light of future discussions with the specialist subcontractor.

Since for BIM Level 2 the exchange of the model is the chief means of communicating design intent holistically, the above revisioning regime is applicable to entire models representing each discipline or specialism. On the more granular scale of specific groups elements, it is important to record within each model any changes that represent this level of consensus.

One useful mechanism for recording consensus within the model is the BIM Coordination File, which was described earlier in this chapter. The issue of these federated coordination models is in addition to the regular exchange of single-discipline models.

Delays in propagating design fixity into the model are probably the most significant hindrance to BIM adding value. Until a design consensus is reflected in the model, the model (which, under the CIC BIM Protocol, takes precedence over information extracted from it) ceases to communicate the entire agreed status of the design. The whole point of BIM is to ensure that project consensus resides in the centrally accessible model, instead of remaining in the traditionally separated and unconnected silos of information retained by each discipline.

CAPTURING DESIGN OPTIONS IN BIM

The impact of design alternatives must be thoroughly reviewed before the project team can arrive at a consensus. There are two key aspects to accomplishing this through a BIM workflow.

1 Revision management

2 Development of design options in the model.

REVISION MANAGEMENT

In fig.8.10 on the facing page, the Architectural Model P01 (in purple) precedes all other disciplines and is placed in the Common Data Environment along with associated drawings and documentation.
This file is downloaded by recipients and linked into the first structural (green) and MEP (yellow) models.

Interim models are issued by each discipline as snapshots of design alternatives or to demonstrate the current state to which the design has progressed. Interim models should use the R01, R02 suffixes as these are for review only.

The issue of structural revision P02 does not precipitate the sharing of immediate corresponding revisions for MEP and Architecture.

All models will undergo work-in-progress versioning to capture changes that represent a milestone or internal design consensus (these marked in grey, these are marked, e.g., P01_1, P01_2, etc.). Introducing another discipline's updated model should also prompt a new version of the main model that includes these updates.

Figure 8.10 Sharing of first architectural revision, P01

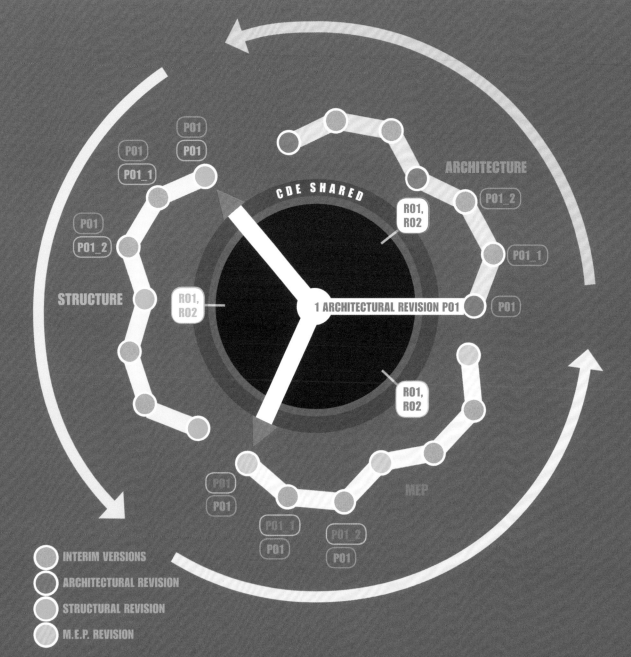

CDE SHARED

ARCHITECTURE

R01,
R02

P01_2

P01_1

P01

STRUCTURE

P01
P01
P01_1

P01
P01_2

R01,
R02

1 ARCHITECTURAL REVISION P01

R01,
R02

MEP

P01
P01

P01_1
P01

P01_2
P01

INTERIM VERSIONS

ARCHITECTURAL REVISION

STRUCTURAL REVISION

M.E.P. REVISION

Figure 8.11 Internal versioning of models after linking to structural and MEP revisions, P02

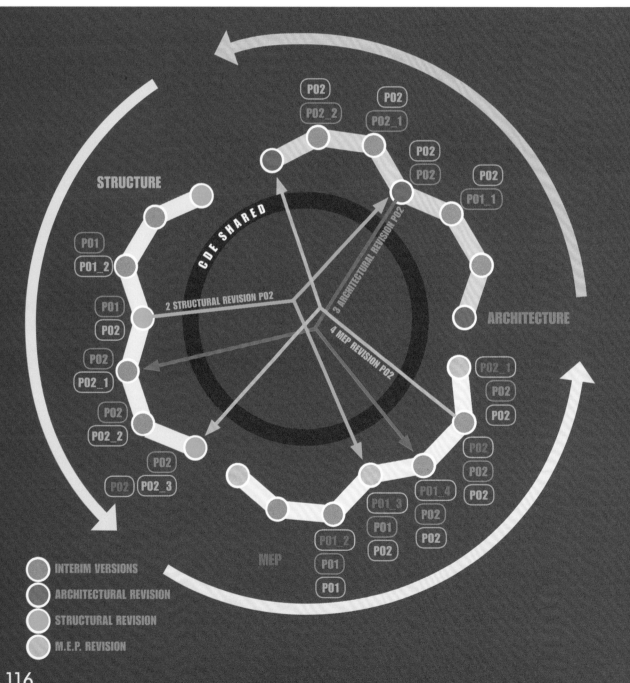

As shown on the facing page (fig 8.11) the MEP model has been simply iterated to the next versions (P01_3, P01_4) until the coordination schedule, a design deadline or the achievement of team consensus prompts the engineers to release their next revision, P02. This model is incorporated into the architectural and structural workstreams by versioning their models with the suffix P02_3.

DEVELOPMENT OF DESIGN OPTIONS IN THE MODEL

Model development workflows can incorporate design options. Once created, each option can be isolated in corresponding views and schedules. In the Autodesk Revit® example below, the cruciform pitched roof is the primary option. ▽

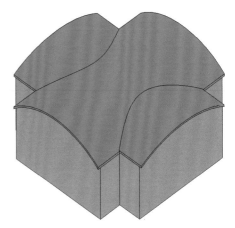

Figure 8.13 Secondary design option – Cruciform barrel roof[4]

△ A cruciform barrel roof has been added to the second design option. The view is duplicated and modified to isolate the barrel roof.

The wall below that is coordinated with the primary option is noticeably uncoordinated with the second:

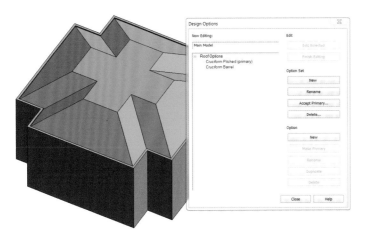

Figure 8.12 Primary design option – Cruciform roof[4]

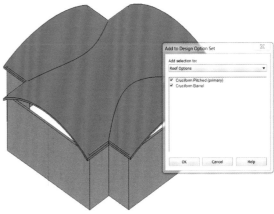

Figure 8.14 Secondary design option – barrel roof coordinated with walls[4]

△ The resolution of this issue requires any connected elements to be duplicated and added to both design options:

117

Figure 8.15 Secondary design option – barrel roof coordinated with walls[4]

△ Sets of walls belonging to each option can now be joined to their corresponding roofs

Cruciform Barrel Roof Schedule	
Family and Type	Area
Basic Roof: Generic-300	123.54 m²
Basic Roof: Generic-300	399.80 m²
Basic Roof: Generic-300	123.53 m²
	646.87 m²

Figure 8.16 Roofing schedule for primary design option[4]

△ The associated schedule can also be set to display data associated with a particular option

Cruciform Pitched Roof Schedule	
Family and Type	Area
Basic Roof: Generic-300	485.31 m²
Basic Roof: Generic-300	115.96 m²
	601.27 m²

Figure 8.17 Roofing schedule for secondary design option

△ Any option can be set to be primary and the primary option can be accepted (once a consensus has been reached), at which stage any other options within that option set will be deleted.

AUTOMATIC DESIGN VERIFICATION IN BIM

The ability to apply automatic rule checking to models is one of the most important developments in BIM software. It heralds a future in which clients will be able to use 'self-service' web-based tools to verify that design work complies with codes and other specified approval criteria.

Rules can be used to check on model integrity, e.g. whether there are duplicate elements that would produce erroneous schedules, or whether all partition types have been updated to those agreed in construction procurement.

Alternatively, the rules can produce a complete inventory of proposed furniture, fixtures and equipment for the intended building.

Industry-recognised tools like Solibri Model Checker® allow users to combine several rules into a ruleset that can be run on an IFC file.

As an example, one of the accessibility requirements rules checks doors in conjunction with associated spaces in the following ways:

Free Door Front Side	This requirement checks on the unobstructed minimum area in front of the door.
Free Door Back Side	This requirement checks on the unobstructed minimum area behind the door.
Free Door Side	This requirement checks on the unobstructed minimum area in front of a swing door, on the side opposite to hinges.
A + B > 2300	This special requirement checks on the overall width and depth of unobstructed minimum area in front of the door

Table 8.1 Rule checks for accessibility requirements[5]

Figure 8.18 Ruleset folders: Solibri Model Checker[*5]

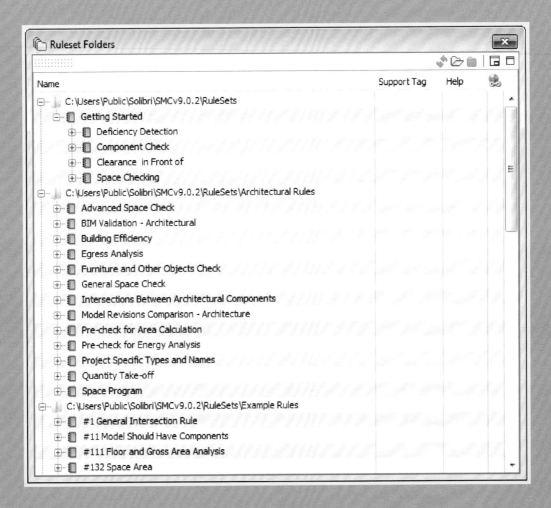

There are also pre-defined rules that can check on ramp and stair accessibility, verify that elements are connected to the defined spaces that enclose them and that perform automatic escape routes analysis.

Figure 8.19 Accessibility requirements ruleset dialogue box – Solibri Model Checker®5

Figure 8.20 Escape route analysis – Solibri Model Checker®5

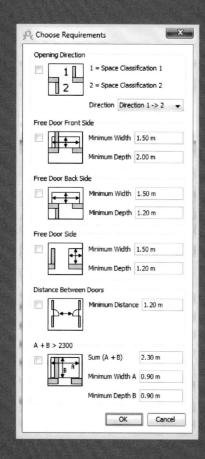

CONCLUSION

The major efficiency improvements promised by BIM will only be realised to the extent that entire project teams adopt the 'best practices' of model-based collaboration. As discussed, there is a wide range of tools and methods available for tracking design and construction issues in the model, for iterating revisions precisely, developing design alternatives and processing models for code and other design criteria compliance.

In order to automate design verification in BIM, it is crucial that models are developed carefully, vetted before issue and then exchanged in accordance with agreed protocol. Adequate time for this must be factored into the design process.

It is likely that it is only a matter of a few years before it becomes commonplace for clients to run code and design criteria checks on uploaded IFC models through a self-service web portal. The advent of this innovation would transform into a reality this aim that is central to the achievement of BIM Level 3.

[1] Copyright © BCFier 2015
[2] Reproduced with permission of BSI Standards limited (BSI).
[3] BS 1192:2007
[4] Autodesk screen shots reprinted with the permission of Autodesk, Inc.
[5] Solibri Model Checker screen shots reprinted with the permission of Solibri Ltd.

09

LEVEL OF DEFINITION PROGRESSION IN BIM

INTRODUCTION

Collaboration is only successful when the scope of each participant's contribution is clearly defined. Before BIM, level of detail was the main gauge of responsibility for developing more specific design intentions in the project drawings and associated data.

For BIM Level 2, the Level of Definition (LOD) extends level of detail to include the quality of information that is either embedded in or linked to different categories of elements in the federated model.

For agreed purposes at each work stage, the LOD should:
- Establish the extent to which, for specified purposes, each project member is contractually obliged to develop elements of the model and embed or link different aspects of design, construction and facilities management information to it.
- Gauge the extent to which elements from each model and their associated data should be relied upon by other members of the project team.

In this chapter, the Model Production and Delivery Table (MPDT) will be explained as a management tool for assigning responsibility to different project members for adding increasingly definitive information and geometric detail to various elements in the 3D model.

3D coordination will also be considered, as it is particularly affected by LOD. This is because those involved in this process must make allowances for the tentative size and positioning of various building components, until they are understood to be definitive.

The key coverage of this chapter is as follows:
- The importance of design sequence to Levels of Definition
- Classifying Levels of Definition
- How LOD affects coordination
- Modelling access and clearances in 3D.

THE IMPORTANCE OF DESIGN SEQUENCE TO LEVELS OF DEFINITION

When a particular level of definition is designated for different types of models and elements, it becomes the basis for interpreting the degree of design intent that they convey, whether conceptual, fully specified, or the final 'as-constructed' representation.

Level of Definition is an estimation that comprises two gauges of design development: the level of detail and the level of information. Whereas level of detail is primarily related to the geometric presentation of model elements, level of information refers to any text and numerical data correlated to those elements.

During the collaborative process, consensus will be achieved for some features of the design significantly earlier than for others. For instance, the structural shop drawings might be ready long before the building services have been detailed for fabrication. It is due to the interdependence of these various systems that the specification is required indicating how LOD should progress over the course of the project.

As another example: as long as ceiling heights are still no more than architectural approximations, heating and cooling loads – which are based on room volumes – cannot be calculated accurately. Similarly, the structural engineer will be unable to calculate the loading on the plant room floor with precision

until the services engineer has specified a particular model of air handling unit.

Therefore, LOD measures how specifically both the geometry and information issued via one party's models and elements can and should be relied upon by other project participants in the design and construction process.

CLASSIFYING LEVELS OF DEFINITION

The numerical values for LOD classify the progression of different categories of elements from tentative to definitive over the course of the project:

LOD	DESCRIPTION
1 – Brief	Model information communicating the brief, performance requirements, performance benchmarks and site constraints.
2 – Concept	Models which communicate the initial response to the brief, aesthetic intent and outline performance requirements The model can be used for early design development, analysis and coordination. Model content is not fixed and may be subject to further design development. The model can be used for coordination, sequencing and estimating purposes.
3 – Developed	A dimensionally correct and coordinated model which communicates the response to the design brief, aesthetic intent and some performance information that can be used for analysis, design development and early contractor engagement. The model can be used for coordination, sequencing and estimating purposes including the agreement of a first stage target price.
4 – Production	A dimensionally correct and coordinated model that can be used to verify compliance with planning and regulatory requirements, and can be used as the start point for the incorporation of specialist contractor design models. The model can be used for coordination, sequencing and estimating purposes, including the agreement of a target price/GMP.
5 – Installation	An accurate model of the asset before and during construction, incorporating coordinated specialist subcontract design models and associated model attributes. The model can be used for coordination of fabrication models, sequencing of installation and capture of as-installed information.
6 - As constructed	An accurate record of the asset as constructed at handover, including all Information required for operation and maintenance.
7 – In use	An updated record of the asset at a fixed point in time incorporating any major changes made since handover, including performance and condition data and all information required for operation and maintenance.

Table 9.1 Levels of definition classifying progression of elements over time from tentative to definitive[1]

Consider the previous example of a building services engineer calculating heating and cooling loads. From the outset of the project, it might have been agreed that, by RIBA stage 3, the ceilings in the architect's model would be at LOD 2. On that basis, the lack of definitive ceiling levels would make the engineer's room volume calculations tentative. As a result, the consequent sizing of air conditioning equipment would be treated as approximate. Level of Definition seeks to generate this kind of common understanding about information exchanged between members of the project team.

LOD also establishes the completeness of the model elements and data required for formal issue to the employer at each gateway decision-point. This is why the Model Production and Delivery Table (below) that specifies LOD for the entire project is structured by 'data drops.'

Figure 9.1 Model Production and Delivery Table (CIC BIM Protocol, Appendix 1)[2]

	Drop 1 Stage 1		Drop 2a Stage 2		Drop 2b Stage 2		Drop 3 Stage 3		Drop 4 Stage 6	
	Model Originator	Level of Detail	Model Originator	Level of Detail	Model Originator	Level of Detail	Model Originator	Level of Detail	Model Originator	Level of Detail
Overall form and content										
Space planning	Architect	1	Architect	2	Contractor	2	Contractor	3	Contractor	6
Site and context	Architect	1	Architect	2	Contractor	2	Contractor	3	Contractor	6
Surveys							Contractor	3		
External form and appearance			Architect	2	Contractor	2	Contractor	3	Contractor	6
Building and site sections					Contractor	2	Contractor	3	Contractor	6
Internal layouts					Contractor	2	Contractor	3	Contractor	6
Design strategies										
Fire			Architect	2	Contractor	2	Contractor	3	Contractor	6
Physical security			Architect	2	Contractor	2	Contractor	3	Contractor	6
Disabled access					Contractor	2	Contractor	3	Contractor	6
Maintenance access			Architect	2	Contractor	2	Contractor	3	Contractor	6
BREEAM					Contractor	2	Contractor	3	Contractor	6
Performance										
Building	Architect	1	Architect	2	Contractor	2	Contractor	3		
Structural	Architect	1	Str Eng	2	Contractor	2	Contractor	3		
MEP systems	Architect	1	MEP Eng	2	Contractor	2	Contractor	3		
Regulation compliance analysis							Contractor	3	Contractor	6
Thermal Simulation							Contractor	3	Contractor	6
Sustainability Analysis							Contractor	3	Contractor	6
Acoustic analysis							Contractor	3	Contractor	6
4D Programming Analysis										
5D Cost Analysis										
Services Commissioning							Contractor	3	Contractor	6
Elements, materials components										
Building			Architect	2	Contractor	2	Contractor	3	Contractor	6
Specifications			MEP Eng	2	Contractor	2	Contractor	3	Contractor	6
MEP systems					Contractor	2	Contractor	3	Contractor	6
Construction proposals										
Phasing							Contractor	3		
Site access							Contractor	3		
Site set-up							Contractor	3		
Health and safety										
Design							Contractor	3		
Construction							Contractor	3		
Operation							Contractor	3	Contractor	6

THE BIM TOOLKIT®: LEVEL OF DETAIL AND LEVEL OF INFORMATION

A progression from the tabulation of model development responsibilities, the BIM Toolkit® is an online management tool that facilitates project data exchange via BIM to the level of definition required for each work stage. Standards for Level of Detail (LoD) and Level of Information (LoI) have been published as part of the BIM Toolkit, aligned to the RIBA / CIC / PAS1192 work stages.

It is intended that these, along with Uniclass 2015 naming conventions, should be adopted as part of the UK Level 2 suite of BIM documents which form a cohesive suite of documentation required for UK Level 2 BIM adoption. The Toolkit assists in both the understanding of these definitions and classification structures and their application on projects across some 9000 building elements.

The Toolkit currently provides over 400 examples of LoD and LoI representations for Architecture, Infrastructure, Landscape Architecture, Civil, Structural and MEP elements across all appropriate work stages. These also provide useful links to the National BIM Library, allowing more direct access to relevant BIM content.

By separating the graphical and geometric definition of BIM Systems and Objects (LoD) from the data attached to these objects (LoI), the Toolkit verifies uploaded BIM data against defined standards of modelling and data completeness. This capability supports several areas of design progression.

As outlined in Chapter 4, the Toolkit provides a suite of project management tools to support the development of a Design Responsibility Matrix. The application of LoD standards means that, from the outset of each work stage, each project participant is aware of the expected geometric definition to be provided for the model elements under their ownership. Consistency in the geometric content of model contributions from all disciplines allows a more rigorous approach to design coordination and clash detection to be used. By consistently applying the Toolkit's LoD, all disciplines will be providing equivalent standards of information. Equally, applying LoD standards to project data generated for all RIBA / CIC / PAS1192 work stages ensures that more uniform geometric and graphical output will be achieved.

The separation of LoD and LoI offers further benefits for model development and information management. By separately defining LoI, the Toolkit effectively confirms the necessary briefing information at an elemental level at the commencement of each work stage. Initially, this will simply confirm requirements against spaces or rooms, which, in later work stages, then informs the development of Systems and Objects that enclose the spaces, e.g. walls, doors, slabs, systems serving spaces etc.

https://toolkit.thenbs.com

Figure 9.2 Level of Detail Principles 2[3]

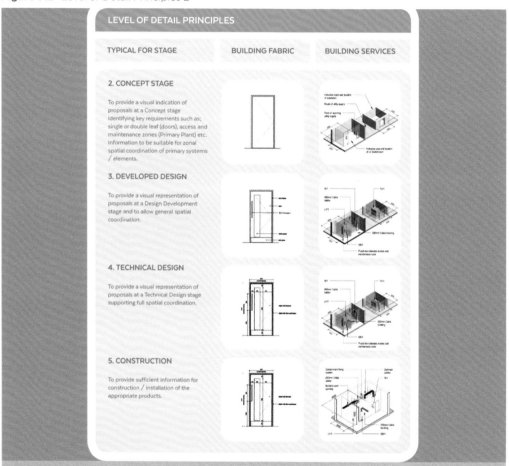

At the end of each work stage, Information Exchanges must then provide the necessary responses to the briefing questions that were asked at the beginning of that stage. The Toolkit assists in a number of areas by providing

- The framework through which LoI is defined.
- Guidance on what information is required at an elemental level for each work stage.
- Checking tools to confirm model outputs against defined deliverables by work stage.
- Ultimately, links to the NBS Create product to assist with more automated specification production.

HOW LOD AFFECTS COORDINATION

LOD can have a real bearing on the ability to resolve coordination issues in BIM and it must be taken into account when checking for clashes or clearances.

For example, at RIBA Stage 2, the model might contain two boilers separated by a clearance of 3 metres. Despite their detailed geometry, the boiler elements should only be interpreted as indicative in specification, location and size at LOD 2.

At Stage 2, if the model was used to review facility management issues, the prospective building manager might highlight access and maintenance issues associated with the 3m clearance between the boilers. At that point in the project, it would be explained that equipment sizes and locations remained tentative, but that the concerns expressed would be recorded as an issue for future resolution (using the BIM coordination file mentioned in Chapter 8).

By RIBA Stage 4, the dimensions of the boilers and distance between them should be resolved since elements at the corresponding LOD 3 can be used to finalise coordination for installation, access and maintenance.

MODELLING ACCESS AND CLEARANCES IN 3D

The required access and clearances should be modelled in addition to 3D geometry of any equipment itself. As an example, the 3D boiler shown on the facing page is derived from the NBS National BIM Library. It has been modelled with a volume that represents its clearance zone.

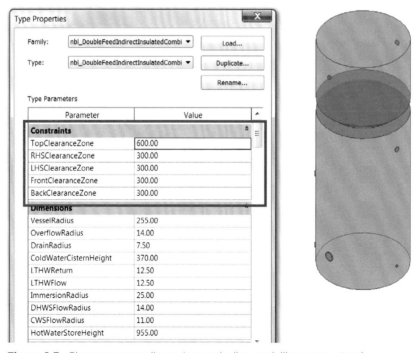

Figure 9.3 Clearance zone dimensions as boiler modelling parameters[4]

The modelled clearance zone can be switched on and tested for interference with other components in the designated 3D coordination review software.

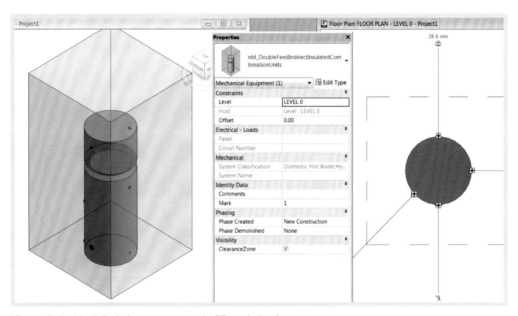

Figure 9.4 Modelled clearance zones in 3D and plan[4]

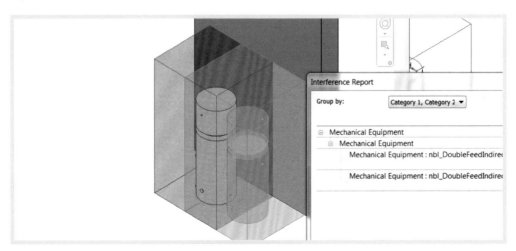

Figure 9.5 Interference between clearance zones detected in the model[4]

CONCLUSION

The level of definition described in PAS-1192 gauges the extent to which elements from each model and their associated data should be relied upon for re-use by other members of the project team. As such, it is primarily aimed at establishing progressive project-wide expectations for using the model.

As an appendix to the BIM Protocol, the Model Production and Delivery Table (MPDT) provides a means of specifying who is responsible during each work stage for the design and required level of definition for the entire range of BIM deliverables. Therefore, it is important for this table to reflect a realistic apportionment of responsibility for progressing model development throughout the project, from the conceptual to the 'as-built' representation of the building.

As a part of the protocol, the MPDT should be reviewed carefully and critically by each firm's BIM Manager. For later project stages, model elements must be re-examined all the more closely to ensure that they represent the agreed level of definition upon which other project team members will rely.

By providing a portal that verifies BIM data against defined standards of modelling and information completeness at each project stage, the BIM Toolkit™ represents a significant advancement on tabular methods of controlling levels of definition.

By adding to each piece of equipment in the model the 3D clearance zones that represent its respective required access and maintenance space, 3D coordination is improved.

In the last chapter, we will explore how to aggregate and hand over the data embedded in the model that will allow the self-same equipment to be maintained.

[1] 1 CIC BIM Protocol (2013) Construction Industry Council
[2] PAS 1192-2:2013, Specification for information management for the capital/delivery phase of construction projects using building information modelling, 2013: British Standards Institution.
[3] Image courtesy of BDP Ltd.
[4] Autodesk screen shots reprinted with the permission of Autodesk, Inc.

10

BIM IN THE
HAND-OVER PHASE

INTRODUCTION

In this final chapter, we consider the transition, by means of BIM, from coordinated project information in the project delivery phase to coordinated asset information in the operational phase.

The concept of the model is expanded beyond the building's graphical representation to include the full array of coherently structured data developed in relation to it. In particular, COBie is the mandatory data structure for formal BIM Level 2 information exchange.

In respect of managing coordinated asset information, we review the publicly available specification, PAS-1992-3[1], which was developed in concert with PAS-1992-2 in order to provide a framework of generic guidance on how the asset information model should be developed from project information model.

The key coverage of this chapter is as follows:
- The importance of information management to operational cost-effectiveness
- What is an information model?
- Organisational information requirements
- Asset information requirements.

THE IMPORTANCE OF INFORMATION MANAGEMENT TO OPERATIONAL COST-EFFECTIVENESS

A much-debated construction industry rule of thumb, first published In the Royal Academy of Engineering paper The *Long Term Costs of Owning and Using Buildings*[2], reads as follows:

'If the initial construction costs of a building is 1, then its maintenance and operating costs over the years is 5, and the business operating costs (salary of people working in that building) is 200.'

The actual ratios can vary with a number of factors (e.g. land cost and the type and location of the building), what is not in dispute is the fact that operation and maintenance costs eventually dwarf those incurred during the design and construction phase. This means that access to reliable structured information

about the former will have a far greater influence on the long-term 'bottom-line' than design and construction expenditure.

PAS-1192-3[1] is the *'specification for information management for the operational phase of construction projects using building information modelling'*. As the document explains of itself: *'this PAS is fundamentally about availability, integrity and transfer of data and information during the operational phase of an asset's life'*.

In respect of the future management of any building, the handover of comprehensive, organised 'as constructed' asset data provides an improved baseline for budgetary decisions. It also forms a register for organising equally comprehensive data on regulatory compliance, maintenance and warranty agreements, suppliers, room inventories, method statements, business continuity impact assessments and health and safety notifications.

WHAT IS AN INFORMATION MODEL?

For data to inform decisions, it must be capable of being searched and sorted by consistently formatted criteria. The information model is the logical organisation of data accumulated and verified over the course of the project in relation to computer-based elements. These elements, whether graphical or text-based, provide a 'real world' context for organising the data. The data itself can be categorised as follows:[2]

- Documents: officially formatted, recorded and change-controlled information, such as correspondence, drawings and schedules.
- Non-graphical information: Pieces of data about an element that are stored as consistently defined attributes, such as specifications and interrelated properties.
- Graphical information: Dimensional data relating to each element and represented as computer-based geometry.

In the broadest terms, the word 'model' goes far beyond just computer graphics and describes the logical organisation of data for the purpose of supporting the owner's decision-making.

As long as its quality and currency is maintained, this logically organised data can be used to assist management in identifying opportunities to better utilise available capacity, to control costs and to provide greater flexibility in accommodating the requirements of the building's occupants.

ORGANISATIONAL INFORMATION REQUIREMENTS

Corporate strategy requires information as the rational basis for guiding the purchase, use, maintenance, and disposal of every asset that an organisation needs in order to maintain and develop its business.

This information should be sufficient to support comprehensive strategic decisions about how best to finance the acquisition of new assets, to maintain existing ones and to dispose of those that have reached the end of their economic life. In particular, organisational information is often required as summarised headlines that can be easily digested, rather than being itemised in fine detail.

As part of the Employer's Information Requirements (see Chapter 2), the Organisational Information Requirements define the type of data that will inform strategic decisions by:

- Comparing the operations and maintenance (O and M) lifecycle costs (at net present value) of alternative capital investments.
- Scheduling all asset replacement values and maintenance costs.
- Assessing the total cost of maintaining (or temporarily deferring maintenance of) a specific asset(s)/asset system.
- Determining the operational and financial impact of asset unavailability or failure.
- Determining the end of economic life of assets/asset systems.
- Identifying the expiry of warranty period and warranty.
- Undertaking financial analysis of planned income and expenditure.
- Undertaking the ongoing identification, assessment and control of asset related risks.
- Complying with statutory and regulatory obligations.

ASSET INFORMATION REQUIREMENTS

There is also a need to provide the more detailed data that will ensure that more immediate operational value is derived from company assets. These Asset Information Requirements (AIRs) are more closely aligned with the day-to-day management of the building.

Typically, AIRs will describe the scope of information that must be developed by coordinating data extracted from 'as constructed' models and verified in order to provide a comprehensive fully populated asset register for the facilities management (FM) team at hand-over. The requirement should include:

- Descriptions of assets, their functions and the asset systems they serve.
- Locations of assets, possibly using spatial referencing or geographical information systems.
- Vendor data, giving details of the organisation that supplied the asset.

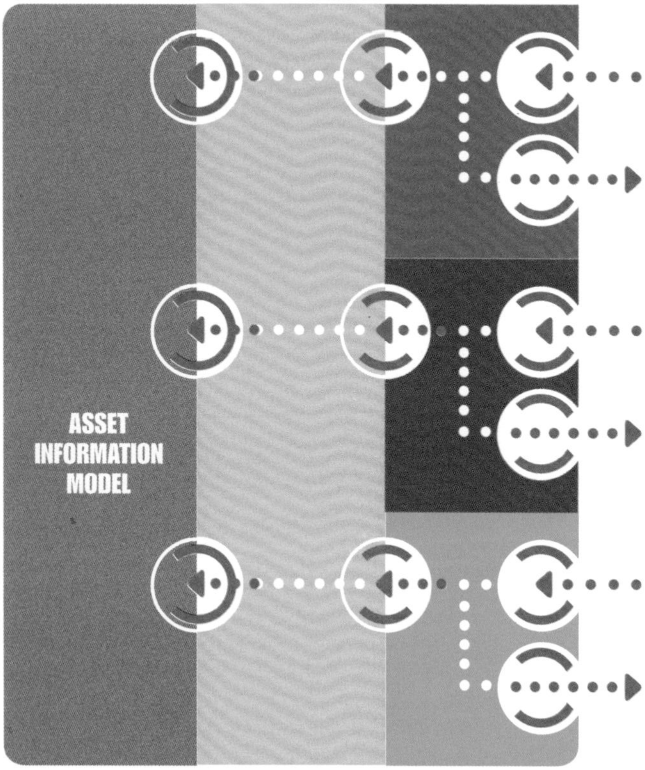

- Operating instructions
- Maintenance instructions such as SFG20 schedules
- Engineering data, design parameters, and engineering drawings
- Fault-finding instructions
- Commissioning instructions
- Commissioning dates and data
- Health and safety files
- Regular statutory test requirements.

It is through BIM Project Execution Plans and Information Delivery Plans (see Chapter 2) that the main contractor defines how data will be developed and collected through the supply chain and tested for quality before issue to the client. The consolidation of data from the sub-models of each sub-contractor is by a process known as model federation (as also described in Chapter 2).

INFORMATION EXCHANGES AND THE PROJECT PROCESS

Instead of simply preparing this accumulated information for final handover, data is extracted throughout the process, from progressively more precisely detailed and information-rich models, and sent to the client at milestones specified in the BIM Project Execution Plan. Issuing organised coherent information in this way is known as information exchange. In PAS-1192-2, an information exchange is described as a *'structured collection of information at one of a number of pre-defined stages of a project with defined format and fidelity'*. The CIC Outline Scope of Services for the role of Information Management describes it as *'configured information delivered from the Information Model for a specific Permitted Purpose.'*

In summary, an information exchange is *'the delivery of data extracted from the model... configured in a format that enables the Employer (and others) to authorise further project development at key project stages.*

ASSET INFORMATION MODEL

Figure 10.1 Common Data Environment Project Information Model is verified and quality checked at handover to become Asset Information Model

The data is generated from the collaborative 3D environment, whereby all related documentation, non-graphical information and graphical information from the entire project team can be assembled into a comprehensive Project Information Model.'

According to Dale Sinclair's *Assembling a Collaborative Project Team,*[3] there are three types of information exchanges:

- Informal 'work-in-progress' information shared between design team members to allow each designer to progress their own design work, to facilitate collaborative working and to allow the lead designer to coordinate the developing design.

- Ad hoc information released to progress a particular topic with third parties (not included in the project team, e.g. local authority, or utility company.

- *'Formal information exchanges... principally at a pause in the design process allowing a period for reflection and sign-off before the next stage commences.'*

When issued, each type of exchange requires all data to be coherent in relation to what is *known* by the project team (rather than what is tentative). This is because BIM allows all project members to reference each other's information for project-related purposes. For example, it would be a serious problem if, at a later design stage and despite using BIM, there was a major disparity between the ceiling heights specified in the architect's room schedule and those in the services engineer's model and schedules used to calculate volume for HVAC loads analysis.

The distinction between what should be relied on as certain and what remains tentative is established by assigning a progressive Level of Definition to different aspects of the issued data. For a given project work stage, this is the extent to which the graphical detail and non-graphical data can be relied upon for different purposes by members of the project team. This is explained in more detail in Chapter 9.

AGGREGATING AND SHARING ASSET DATA

The development of the Project Information Model (see Chapter 2) must be managed over the entire project lifecycle, issued to the client in the form of data drops at the specified intervals, and finally verified at handover to become the Asset Information Model.

A checking regime must be established that ensures that:

- The model contains elements that are representative of every maintainable asset in the proposed building.

- Asset data (itemised in the above section on AIRs) is being added to all model elements.

This data must be refined in order to represent eventually accurate 'as constructed' information on the full complement of assets that comprise the completed building works.

Instead of opening the 3D model, the client and other stakeholders can derive considerable value from reviewing the development of the evolving Project Information Model as standardised 'snapshots' which tabulate the key properties of the assets intended for the proposed building. For BIM Level 2, PAS-1192-2 and PAS-1192-4[4] mandate the use of the internationally recognised and non-proprietary data structure (i.e. schema) known as Construction Operations Building Information Exchange (or, as specified for the UK, COBie-UK-2012). This can be imported into a wide range of compatible FM software.

COBIE

COBie provides a means of digitally exchanging structured, progressively more definitive asset information for the design, construction and hand-over phases.

The majority of BIM software vendors provide tools for exporting this data directly from the model. Although the commonest approved output is an Excel spreadsheet, there are other approved file formats, such as ifcXML.

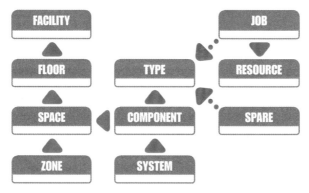

Figure 10.3 The COBie data structure[7]

Each tab on the COBie spreadsheet is assigned to record different types of interrelated asset data.

For each project work stage, there is a progression in the level of information issued to the client via this COBie spreadsheet.

INFORMATION	COBIE SHEET TAB(S)
Spaces and equipment	Space, Type, Component
Space and equipment properties	Attribute
Planned preventive maintenance schedules	Job
Safety procedures	Job
Systems	System
System procedures	Job
Materials, tools, training	Resource
Associated documents	Job
Replacement parts	Spare

Table 10.1 Assignment of asset information types to COBie spreadsheet tabs

COBie Drop 1: Requirement and constraints (room data sheets)

COBie Drop 2: Outline solution

COBie Drop 3: Construction Information

COBie Drop 4: Operation and maintenance

COBie Drop 5 (or more): Operation and maintenance post occupancy

Model Integrity

As a word of warning, it is important to establish a regime for maintaining model integrity, especially in respect of exporting COBie data that will be issued to the client. Model integrity refers to the accuracy and consistency of elements and associated data that comprise the model. If the model contains extraneous or duplicated elements, its exported data (including COBie) cannot reliably represent design intent or construction information for a particular work stage.

In order to identify anomalies, regular visual scrutiny of extracted worksheets should be coupled with the use of either an add-on or dedicated model checking application (such as Solibri Model Checker®). The latter provides a set of automatic rules that can eliminate the above-mentioned discrepancies from the model before export to COBie.

Government Soft Landings and FM Workshops

COBie data provides not only a consistently organised summary for end-users to assess how the project is meeting the requirements in the brief, but also, once verified, an asset database for handover to FM. As such, its data is invaluable for early engagement with end-users on how the design will meet the specified requirements, as well as for post-construction after-care.

Government Soft Landings (GSL) is a major public policy that encourages end-users to engage with the project delivery process at every stage, from design to construction to hand-over and post-occupancy. It was established by the UK government to *'improve performance of buildings and to meet the requirements of those that use them'*.[5]

Beyond project delivery, a stated guiding principle of GSL policy is that 'Building Information Modelling (BIM) will provide a fully populated asset data set to feed into

RIBA WORK STAGE	GSL POTENTIAL FOR INFORMATION FROM BIM AND COBIE
0 – Strategic Definition 1 – Brief	Agree required asset database format with FM team, and appoint Information Manager to implement written policies on their scheduled collection from the project team (Information Delivery Plans). From the briefing database, generate room datasheets that capture requirements. Hold workshops to validate requirements.
2 – Concept 3 – Developed Design 4 – Technical Design	**COBie Drop 1** - Stakeholder FM workshops to check room layouts and adjacencies, room data sheets and COBie gross internal floor areas (GIFAs) against schedule of accommodations and performance benchmarks in the brief. Involve future facility managers in model walkthroughs to evaluate usability, including proposed plant and controls locations. Use GIFAs for capital expenditure (CAPEX) cost analysis. Use **initial baseline energy model** for BREEAM and operating expenditure (OPEX) predictions. Use component and systems worksheets to begin scoping and refining the contractual requirement for pre-hand-over procedures, logbooks and user guides. **COBie Drop 2** – COBie Component worksheet and comprehensive Equipment Responsibilities Matrix used for cost analysis, package scope and budget review in conjunction with suppliers. Predicted consumption generated from **final baseline energy model** at financial close.
5 – Construction	**COBie Drop 3** – Sort components worksheet by space and use to develop planned preventive maintenance (PPM) strategy. Generate equipment checklists and review site/systems orientation training checklists with contractor on behalf of commissioning and premises team. Test and verify import of asset data into CAFM.
6 – Handover	**COBie Drop 4** – Involve commissioning team in verification of collated and finalised COBie worksheets. Once complete, import asset data into CAFM. Collate test data records during commissioning process.
7 – In use	**COBie Drop 5** (or more) – As part of post-occupancy evaluation, sub-metered energy reports and controls data are used to develop the in-use energy model as a 'reality-check' of earlier design assumptions. Exported data from CAFM may be linked into regularly updated 'as constructed' 3D models in readiness for future refurbishment, extension and de-commissioning works.

Table 10.2 Stakeholder engagement through COBie data for Government Soft Landings

Computer Aided Facilities Management (CAFM) system. This data will need to be maintained throughout the building life cycle. The Cabinet Office documentation on GSL notes that, on government projects, this aspect of the guidance is mandatory and must be followed to comply with the policy.

A Soft Landings Champion is appointed to spearhead early end-user engagement with the project team during design and construction. Part of this engagement includes FM workshops aimed at evaluating the eventual usability of the asset, and preparations for hand-over as the intended facility evolves in design.

Table 10.2 contains a number of key examples that show how information derived from BIM, including COBie, should be used during each project work stage.

Thus, the COBie worksheets should be used in combination with other design information as a valuable progress check. Nevertheless, it may be necessary to establish a more direct workflow for collating and publishing asset data from supply chain models into CAFM after verification by the Soft Landings team.

The long-term value of digital transfer from the federated model to CAFM is that it eliminates much of the cost and time involved in collating FM data through major post-project asset auditing. As described in the Facilities Management Service Standards within the Central Government Office Estate[6], if completed properly, this process will deliver a comprehensive *'asset list of all plant and equipment which can be kept regularly updated – to a level applicable for performing routine maintenance (PPM) and also undertaking full condition/ remaining life surveys on all built assets (in scope).'*

While there is a growing list of Computer Aided Facilities Management (CAFM) software that is capable of importing COBie data, the BIM Manager should hold workshops with the FM team to identify and test other formats (such as IFC). Alternative data translation workflows (using software, such as FME Desktop®) may be needed to export from them reliably into the Employer's CAFM System.

CONCLUSION

Beyond the production of conventional project outputs, COBie data is now an important BIM Level 2 expectation of the employer. In order to maintain the quality of this data throughout the supply chain, a regime must be instituted to regularly audit all sub-models for extraneous and duplicated elements.

Before exporting to COBie, information quality must be checked by designers. They should scrutinise all relevant BIM schedules that relate to their specialties. Also, after training and documenting the process for the supply chain, and in readiness for 'data drops', trial runs of the full COBie export should be conducted. These should involve testing the process of aggregating this exported data from the entire supply chain.

The BIM Manager should also conduct workshops throughout the project with the Soft Landings Champion and FM team to ensure that the trial COBie data can be imported into the CAFM system without data omissions or errors. If the system is not COBie-compatible, alternative data translation tools, such as FME Desktop®, may be required.

In accordance with the BIM Project Execution Plan, BIM Managers should establish a project delivery check-list of model set-up, standardised production processes and implementing quality control for all deliverables.

[1] PAS 1192-3:2013, Specification for information management for the operational phase of construction projects using building information modelling, 2013 (British Standards Institution)

[2] Evans, R., Haryott, R., Haste, N. and Jones, A., *The Long Term Costs of Owning and Using Buildings*, 1998 (London: Royal Academy of Engineering)

[3] Dale Sinclair, *Assembling a collaborative project team*, 2013

[4] PAS 1192-4:2014, Collaborative production of information Part 4: Fulfilling employer's information exchange requirements using COBie, Code of practice, 2014 (British Standards Institution).

[5] Government Soft Landings, Section 1, Cabinet Office, April 2013 ©Crown Copyright, p.2

[6] Belinda Mather-Derrick, *Facilities Management Service Standards within the Central Government Office Estate*, 2012, p.25

[7] East, E. William (2012) "Construction-Operations Building information exchange (COBie)," buildingSMART alliance, National Institute of Building Sciences, Washington, DC.

CONCLUSION

In this handbook, I have sought, with the input of other contributors, to provide coherent and comprehensive guidance on the practical implications of managing BIM in readiness for the 2016 government mandate.

This book has drawn extensively upon official standards and other documentation produced by a host of industry experts and government advisory groups, including the BIM Task Group. The advice provided has ranged from the early reminder that BIM strategy should be aligned with client priorities to assessing the practical implications of a phased BIM Level 2 implementation.

This book is not meant to be prescriptive. Instead, the approach has been to provide a range of important issues to consider and corollaries for each organisation to apply.

It will be particularly important for each organisation to reflect on these issues and corollaries and to establish carefully their own consensus on the pace and extent of BIM adoption. This reflective self-paced approach will enable them to achieve not only the immediate improvements in design and coordination that are attributable to BIM, but also the long-term client benefits that are realised through comprehensive, spatially organised asset data.

Although the prospect and aspirations of BIM Level 3 may appear daunting to many, it represents the logical progression towards a built environment economy in which completely digital transactions predominate.

It is this transition to a built environment digital economy that heralds an era in which order of magnitude improvements over conventional project delivery and asset management processes will become commonplace.

GLOSSARY

AIM: Asset Information Model is developed during RIBA stages 5–7 to include all as installed components and systems operational data to support the management and operation of the facility in use.

AIR: Asset Information Requirements set out the post construction information requirements to be delivered within the model and any other data record such as COBie.

BIM: Building Information Modelling Dimensions

- 3D - Model
- 4D – Time
- 5D – Cost and Quantities
- 6D – Facilities Management.

BEP: Building Information Model Execution Plan produced to outline the project protocols, standards and procedures and managing the delivery of the project information

CAD: Computer Aided Design/Drawing

CDE: Common data environment, an information management system and process forming part of the Standards Methods and Procedures outlined within BS1192: 2007. More commonly defined as a single source of information to collate and manage project documentation such as a web based system or a project extranet.

CI/SfB, Construction Industry/ Samarbetskomitten for Byggnadsfragor, combines a UK and Swedish approach to construction classification. The system has been in use for a number of years, and, whilst CI/SfB is being replaced by Uniclass, it can still be found for organising collections in many libraries.

COBie Construction Operations Building Information Exchange identifies the non-geometric information that is needed in order to exchange managed asset information over the life of a project which is typically presented in a spreadsheet format.

Data: unorganised facts stored but not yet interpreted or analysed.

Data Drop: The release of defined information in accordance with the development of the project as set out within the employer's information requirements (EIRs). Compliance with a BIM maturity of Level 2 requires all data drops to be in accordance with COBie standards.

dPOW: the digital plan of work sets out the project workflow and requirements as outlined in a number of UK Government BIM standards and protocols. The concept has been further developed by the NBS within a free to use web based BIM toolkit which enables the project to:

'*define the team, responsibilities and an information delivery plan for each stage of a project.*'

DRM: Design Responsibility Matrix sets out the information requirements for each stage aligned with who will be producing them. A DRM tool can be downloaded from **http://www.ribaplanofwork.com**

DWG file format: can allow any competent CAD operator/technician to measure and review and also make modifications and updates to reflect any changes made during the handover period and in use stage.

DWF file format: allows the same level of interrogation of the information as a .dwg however they are more compressed and typically smaller. This format is not editable.

EIR: Employers Information Requirement's set out what information the client needs to ensure that the design is developed appropriately for the construction and operation of the completed project. This document will accompany the Project Brief.

PDF file format: These have a relatively small file size, and a PDF reader is readily available to download if not already installed on the FM team and Client organisations systems. PDF's cannot be updated.

INDEX

Page numbers in italic indicate figures or tables and in bold indicate glossary terms.

3D *see* BIM Level 2
4D animations 75–8
5D quantification 78–9

access modelling 129–30, *129*, *130*
AIM *see* Asset Information Model (AIM)
AIR *see* Asset Information Requirements (AIR)
animations, 4D 75–8
area data sheets (ADS) 11–12, *12*
assessment attributes 45–6
asset costs 12–13
asset information 14–15, 137–40, *138*, *139*
Asset Information Model (AIM) *136*, 137, **144**
Asset Information Plan 32
Asset Information Requirements (AIR) 135–6, **144**
asset management strategy 8–12
assets 88–9
automated purchasing 59
automatic design verification 118–20, *119*, *120*
awareness campaigns 86

backups 47–8, *47*, *48*
BCF *see* BIM Collaboration Format (BCF)
BCIS *see* Building Cost Information Service (BCIS)
BEPs *see* BIM Execution Plans (BEPs)
Bew-Richards BIM maturity diagram 52–3, *53*
BIM adoption 41–3, *42*, 60–2
BIM capability assessment 48–9
BIM Champion 33, 40–1, 44, 77, 85, 86, 89
BIM Collaboration File 112, 114
BIM Collaboration Format (BCF) 111 2, *111*, *112*
BIM Coordinator 32, 33, 74, 75, 92
BIM deliverables 26, *26*
BIM Execution Plans (BEPs) 72, 91, 103, 136, **144**
    post-contract 30–3
    pre-contract 22–30, *23*
BIM implementation 83–8
    characteristics of success 38
    goals and objectives 60–2
    measuring success 61–2
    organisational BIM assessment 48–9
    precursors to BIM Level 2 40–8, 84
    readiness assessment 84–5

    tasks 85
    tiered approach 38, *39*
BIM implementation plan 85
BIM Information Manager 28, 32, 33, *87*, 97, 98, 99, *139*
BIM Level 0 38, *39*, *52*, 53–4, *53*
BIM Level 1 38, *39*, *52*, *53*, 54
BIM Level 2 18–19, 24, 25, 38, *39*, *52*, *53*, 55–7, 55
    challenges of transition to 57
    goals and objectives 60–1
    organisational assessment 48–9
    precursors to 40–8, 84
BIM Level 3 38, *39*, *52*, *53*, 57–60, *58*, *60*
BIM Manager
    FM workshops 140
    hiring dedicated 75, 88, 89–90
    project delivery task list 91–3
    responsibilities 21–2, 24–5, 27, 32, 33, 46, 57, 77, 79, 131
BIM Maturity Levels 38, *39*, *52*–60, 52, *53*
    Level 0 38, *39*, *52*, 53–4, *53*
    Level 1 38, *39*, *52*, *53*, 54
    Level 3 38, *39*, *52*, *53*, 57–60, *58*, *60*
    see also BIM Level 2
BIM objectives 14, 60–2
BIM Protocol 27, *27*, 28, 30, 98–9, 101
BIM schedules 71–2, *71*, 73
BIM software 24, 30, 41–2, 48, 55–7
    4D animations 75–8
    computer-assisted coordination 70–2, *71*
    computer automated coordination 67–70, *67*, *68*, *69*, *70*
BIM Sponsor 40–1, *42*, 77, 84, 85, 86
BIM strategy 8–13, 14–15, 84
BIM Task Group 18
BIM Technical Adviser 20, 22
BIM Toolkit 28, 127–8, *128*
BIM vision statements 84
BIM Working Party 18, 19, 52, 53
BS-1192 46, *46*, 47, 48, 54
budget 85
building contracts 97–8, 99–101
Building Cost Information Service (BCIS) 13
Building Information Modelling (BIM)
    defined 8
    key benefits 25, 61
business process automation 59

CAD *see* Computer Aided Design (CAD)
capital expenditure (CAPEX) 12, *139*

care, duties of 96–7, 99
CDE *see* Common Data Environment (CDE)
change management 86–7
CI/SfB (Construction Industry/
Samarbetskomitten for Byggnadsfragor) **144**
Cialdini, Robert 40
CIC *see* Construction Industry Council (CIC)
clash avoidance 74–5
clash detection 74–5, 100, 103
classification systems 28, 44, 79, 127
clearance zone modelling 129–30, *129*, *130*
client push *see* push-pull strategy
client strategy 8–13
COBie *see* Construction Operations Building
Information Exchange (COBie)
commercial requirements *20*
Common Data Environment (CDE) 24, 30–1,
54, 74, **144**
    information exchanges 28, 108–10, *109*,
    110, *111*
Computer Aided Design (CAD) 41, 46, 47,
53–4, **144**
Computer Aided Facilities Management
(CAFM) systems 139, 140
computer-assisted coordination 70–2, *71*
computer automated coordination 67–70,
67, 68, 69, 70
construction coordination 70–1, 75–8
Construction Industry Council (CIC) 26
    see also BIM Protocol
Construction Operations Building
Information Exchange (COBie) 103, 137–8,
138, *139*, 140, **144**
Construction Project Information Committee
(CPIC) 8
consultant appointments 97–8
contracts 97–8, 99–101
contractual duties of care 96–7, 99
Cookham Wood Trial Project 102–3
coordination
    challenges 66
    clash avoidance 74–5
    computer-assisted 70–2, *71*
    computer automated 67–70, *67, 68, 69, 70*
    construction sequence 70–1, 75–8
    design coordination processes 47–8, *48*
    errors 66–7, 72–3, *72*
    and Level of Definition 129
    preparation for 74
    roles 73–4

cost analysis 13, 14, 78–9, *139*
cost reductions 84
Costs, Whole Life 12–13, *13*
CPIC *see* Construction Project Information
Committee (CPIC)
CPix BIM Assessment forms 48–9

data 56–7, *56*, 135, **145**
data attributes 44–6, *44, 45*
data corruption liability 99, 101
data drops 33, *34*, 92, *110*, 126, *126*, **145**
data repositories see Common Data
Environment (CDE)
data storage naming protocol 46, *46*
    see also file naming conventions
design coordination processes 47–8, *48*
design fixity 113–14
design intent model 29, 76
design options 117–18, *117*, *118*
design publication standards 43
Design Responsibility Matrix (DRM) 127, **145**
design verification 118–20, *119*, *120*
Digital Built Britain strategy 59–60, *60*
dPOW (digital plan of work) **145**
DRM *see* Design Responsibility Matrix (DRM)
duties of care 96–7, 99
DWF file format **145**
DWG file format **145**

early warning 100
Elemental Standard Form of Cost Analysis
(SFCA) 13, 78
Employer's Information Requirements (EIRs)
19–22, *19, 20, 21*, 135, **145**
end-user support 88
enterprise resource planning systems
(ERPs) 56

facilities management (FM)
    Computer Aided Facilities Management
    (CAFM) systems 139, 140
    workshops *139*, 140
federated model 27–8, *27*, 30, 56
file formats 24, 30, **145**
file naming conventions 30, 46, *46*, 47–8,
48, 54, 74, 108
financial strength 89
fitness for purpose 96
FM *see* facilities management (FM)

gateways 13, 33
global unique IDs (GuIDs) 112

Government Construction Strategy 18–19, 25, 102
Government Soft Landings (GSL) 101, 139–40, *139*

human resources 89–90
   see also organisational structure; roles and responsibilities

in-house learning content 90
Industry Foundation Classes (IFC) 57, 59, 60, 110, 112
influence 40
Information Delivery Plans 31–2, *32*, 92, 136
information exchanges 136–7
   in BIM Toolkit 128
   in Common Data Environment 28, 108–10, *109, 110, 111*
   Construction Operations Building Information Exchange (COBie) 103, 137–8, *138, 139,* 140, **144**
   data drops 33, *34,* 92, *110,* 126, *126,* **145**
   work-in-progress (WIP) 108–10, *109, 110,* 137
information management 31–3
Information Manager *see* BIM Information Manager
information models 135
   see also Asset Information Model (AIM); Project Information Model (PIM)
intellectual property rights 27, 101, 103
Interface Manager *87*
interfaces, proprietary 56
interoperability of models 30
issue tracking systems 43–4

King Abdullah University of Science and Technology (KAUST) project 75–6, *76*

Last Responsible Moment (LRM) decision-making 113–14
layer naming conventions 30, 54
Lead Designer *87*
leadership roles 40–1, 42
'Lessons Learned' sessions 89
Level of Definition (LOD) 124–6, *125,* 129
Level of Detail (LoD) standards 28, 101, 127, *128*
Level of Information (LoI) standards 28, 127
liability, limits of 97, 99, 101
library objects 44–5, *44*
licensing of BIM models 98–9, 101, 103
Life Cycle Costs 12–13, *13*
limits of liability 97, 99, 101

LOD *see* Level of Definition (LOD)
LoD *see* Level of Detail (LoD) standards
LoI *see* Level of Information (LoI) standards
LRM *see* Last Responsible Moment (LRM) decision-making

management 83–8
management requirements *20*
Master Information Delivery Plan (MIDP) 31, 32
material quantity schedules 72, 78–9
matrix of responsibilities 30, *31*
   see also Design Responsibility Matrix (DRM)
MIDP *see* Master Information Delivery Plan (MIDP)
milestones 14, 26, *26*
model federation 27–8, *27,* 30, 56
model integrity 138
model interoperability 30
Model Production and Delivery Table (MPDT) 27, *27,* 30, 32, 99, 100, 126, *126,* 131
model revisions 47–8, 112–13
   review only revisions 113, *113*
   revision file naming 47–8, 113, *113*
   revision management 114–17, *115, 116*
model snapshots 112
Moore, Geoffrey A. 41, *41*
MPDT see Model Production and Delivery Table (MPDT)

NBS Create tool 45, *45*
NBS National BIM Library 44–5, *44*

open BIM workflows 110–13, *111, 112, 113*
operating expenditure (OPEX) 12, *139*
operation and maintenance systems 101
operations and maintenance (O and M) costs 10–11, *10,* 13, 134, 135
organisational BIM assessment 48–9
organisational culture 82–3
Organisational Information Requirements 135
Organisational Process Assets 89
organisational structure 85, 86, *87,* 88

parameters *see* data attributes
PAS-55 14–15
PAS-1192 19, 24–5
PAS-1192-2 19, 22, 28–9, *29,* 30, 32, 33, 56, 73–4, 76–7, 113, *113,* 136
PAS-1192-3 131
PAS-1192-4 137
PDF file format **145**
Personal Development Plans 89

pilot projects 85, 86
PIM *see* Project Information Model (PIM)
Plain Language Questions (PLQs) 21, *21*, *29*, 33, *34*
Pre-Qualification Questionnaires 48–9
procurement models 101–2
project data management systems 43–4
Project Delivery Manager *87*
project delivery task list 91–3
project documentation 43
project goals 25
Project Information Manager *87*
Project Information Model (PIM) 26–7, 28–9, 137
Project Information Plan 26–7, 32
project management software 75, 76, 77
Project Manager 22, 77
Project Outputs 32
proprietary interfaces 56
purchasing, automated 59
push-pull strategy 18, 19–20, *19*

quantification 78–9

readiness assessment 84–5
reasonable endeavours 99
reasonable skill and care *96*, *97*, *99*
responsibility matrix 30, *31*
   see also Design Responsibility Matrix (DRM)
review only revisions 113, *113*
revision file naming 47–8, 113, *113*
revision management 114–17, *115*, *116*
RIBA Plan of Work 21, 102, *139*
risk assessment 22
risk management 100
roles and responsibilities 24, 30, 33, 85, *87*, 88
   BIM Champion 33, 40–1, 44, 77, 85, 86, 89
   BIM Coordinator 32, 33, 74, 75, 92
   BIM Information Manager 28, 32, 33, *87*, 97, 98, 99, *139*
   BIM Sponsor 40–1, 42, 77, 84, 85, 86
   BIM Technical Adviser 20, 22
   coordination roles 73–4
   leadership roles 40–1, 42
   technical coordinators 71, 73, 74, 75, 90, 92
rule checking 118–20, *119*, *120*

schedule of accommodation 11–12, *11*, 78
SFCA *see* Standard Form of Cost Analysis (SFCA)

shared building model 57–9, *58*
simulation attributes 46
small to medium enterprises (SMEs) 40, 75, 88
SMART objectives 14, 61
Soft Landings *see* Government Soft Landings (GSL)
spatial coordination *see* coordination
spatial coordination meetings 74, 75
specification attributes 45
standard form building contracts 97–8, 99–101
Standard Form of Cost Analysis (SFCA) 13, 78
Standard Method and Procedure 24, 27, 30
status codes 74, 113, *113*
sub-models 28, *28*, 91, 93
suggestion box 83
supplier BIM/IT assessment 24–5
supplier pull *see* push-pull strategy
survey strategy 31

Task Information Delivery Plans (TIDPs) 31, 32, *32*, 92
Task Information Manager *87*
task team interface managers *see* technical coordinators
Task Team Manager *87*
technical coordinators 71, 73, 74, 75, 90, 92
technical requirements *20*
technology adoption 41–3, *41*, *42*
TIDPs *see* Task Information Delivery Plans (TIDPs)
tiered investment in BIM 38, *39*
time dimension 75
   see also 4D animations
training 41, 43, 83, 86, 89–90
'Two Stage Open Book' procurement model 102

Uniclass 28, 44, 79, 127

versioning 47, 114–17, *116*
view templates *69*, *70*, 73
virtual construction model 29, 76
Volume Strategy 28, 30

Whole Life Costs 12–13, *13*
work-in-progress (WIP) information exchanges 108–10, *109*, *110*, 137

IMAGE CREDITS

Name	Page
BCFier 2015	111 (bottom), 112 (both)
Image courtesy of BDP Ltd.	128
BSI [1]	13, 29, 46 (top), 113 (top)
Autodesk screen shots reprinted with the permission of Autodesk, Inc.	44, 47, 48 (top), 68-72, 117-118, 129-130
Construction Industry Council	126
Courtesy of Cornwall Council	12
Crown Copyright	11, 60
Robert Eadie et al. [2]	42
Courtesy of Gehry Technologies and HOK	76 (top)
HOK	iv (all), 28, 36, 50, 64, 76 (bottom), 80, 94
HOK, with thanks to Chris Ansell	6, 16, 122, 132
HOK/Chris Wadsworth	106
Kaj A. Jørgensen et al. [3]	55, 58
Mervyn Richards/Mark Bew	53
David Shepherd	10, 19, 23, 39, 46 (middle, bottom), 48 (bottom), 56, 67, 83, 109, 110, 111 (top), 113 (bottom), 115, 116, 136, 138
RIBA	21
RIBA Enterprises Ltd.	45
Solibri Model Checker screen shots reprinted with the permission of Solibri Ltd	119-120

[1] Permission to reproduce extracts from British Standards is granted by British Standards Limited (BSI). No other use of this material is permitted. British Standards can be obtained in PDF or hard copy formats from the BSI online shop: www.bsigroup.com/Shop

[2] Robert Eadie et al., 'An Analysis of the Drivers for Adopting BIM', 2013 ITcon Vol. 18

[3] Kaj A. Jørgensen, Jørn Skauge, Per Christiansson, Kjeld Svidt, Kristian Birch Sørensen and John Mitchell, 'Use of IFC Model Servers: Modelling Collaboration Possibilities in Practice', Aalborg University 2008